SOUTH-WESTERN

Microsoft® Visual Basic® .NET Introduction to Programming, Second Edition

ACTIVITIES WORKBOOK

Michael Sprague

Chicago Public Schools

THOMSON

COURSE TECHNOLOGY

Australia • Canada • Mexico • Singapore • Spain • United Kingdom • United States

THOMSON

COURSE TECHNOLOGY

Microsoft® Visual Basic® .NET, Introduction to Programming, Second Edition
by Michael Sprague

Managing Editor:
Chris Katsaropoulos

Senior Product Manager:
Dave Lafferty

Associate Product Manager:
Jodi Dreissig

Editorial Assistant:
Jordan Casey

Marketing Manager:
Kim Ryttel

Print Buyer:
Laura Burns

Production Editor:
Elena Montillo

**Fee Writer and
Development Editor:**
Custom Editorial Productions
Inc. (CEP)

Cover Design:
Abby Scholz

Compositor:
GEX Publishing Services

Printer:
WebCom Limited

Contents

Unit 1: Mastering the Basics 1
   Lesson 1: The Basics 2
   Lesson 2: Forms and Decisions 11
   Lesson 3: Menus, MDIs, and Simple Loops 21
   Lesson 4: Decisions, Looping, Arrays, and Searching 31
   Unit 1 Review 43

Unit 2: Collections . . . . **.49**
   Lesson 5: Improving the User Interface 50
   Lesson 6: Database Programming 61
   Lesson 7: Debugging and Simple Classes .71
   Lesson 8: Classes and Objects 81
   Lesson 9: Exploring All Kinds of Collections 91
   Unit 2 Review 101

Unit 3: Creating and Using New Controls . . . . **.105**
   Lesson 10: Using Special Controls to Enhance the User Interface 106
   Lesson 11: Building and Using a User Control 119
   Unit 3 Review 135

**Unit 4: Organizing Data, Providing Help, and Building Applications
   for the Internet** . . . . **.139**
   Lesson 12: Stacks and Lists 140
   Lesson 13: Graphics, Help, and Deployment 153
   Lesson 14: Creating Web Projects 169
   Unit 4 Review 177

UNIT 1: MASTERING THE BASICS

LESSON 1   **THE BASICS**

LESSON 2   **FORMS AND DECISIONS**

LESSON 3   **MENUS, MDIs, AND SIMPLE LOOPS**

LESSON 4   **DECISIONS, LOOPING, ARRAYS, AND SEARCHING**

UNIT 1 REVIEW

LESSON 1   THE BASICS

TRUE/FALSE

Circle T if the statement is true or F if the statement is false.

T   F   1. Visual Basic is only intended for experienced programmers to use.

T   F   2. A GUI lets a person use both text and graphics to communicate with the computer.

T   F   3. The Visual Basic prebuilt objects make it easy for novice programmers to create useful programs quickly.

T   F   4. Jobs for Visual Basic programmers are few and far between.

T   F   5. Programmers of Windows applications should follow the established conventions for what basic features to put in their application.

T   F   6. An experienced user of Microsoft applications would expect that the File menu in the Visual Basic program contains many of the same options as the File menu in Microsoft Word.

T   F   7. A Visual Basic project typically has only one file associated with it.

T   F   8. All the files related to a Visual Basic program you write should be contained in a single, unique folder.

T   F   9. It is the programmer's responsibility to make sure the program meets the needs of a variety of users.

T   F   10. Extensions are an optional way to keep track of what type of information is contained in a file.

T   F   11. Labels are used to allow the program user to enter text into the application.

T   F   12. When an action happens in an application, Windows sends a message to the application.

T   F   13. There is very little help available to the Visual Basic programmer.

T   F   14. The only time you need to save your project files is just before you close the Visual Basic program.

MULTIPLE CHOICE

Select the best response for the following statements.

1. The informational box that appears when your mouse pointer rests over a control is called a(n)
   a. Standard toolbar.
   b. ToolTip.
   c. pointer.
   d. InfoBox.
   e. box.

2. The IDE component that contains tools for creating controls to be used on a form in a Visual Basic application is the
   a. Standard toolbar.
   b. ToolTip.
   c. Toolbox.
   d. ToolShelf.
   e. Tool menu.

3. The window that lists all the forms and modules used in a particular project is the
   a. Properties window.
   b. IDE window.
   c. Forms window.
   d. Solution Explorer window.
   e. Component window.

4. A property that can be set using the Properties window is
  a. an object's color.
  b. an object's name.
  c. an object's size.
  d. an object's position.
  e. all of the above

5. If the Toolbox is not open when you start Visual Basic,
  a. you need to call your system support group or help desk.
  b. you have a faulty version of Visual Basic.
  c. you need to exit Visual Basic and restart it.
  d. you need to set your personal Visual Basic preferences to include showing the Toolbox.
  e. you need to click the View menu, and then click the Toolbox option.

6. GUI is an acronym for
  a. generic user interface.
  b. generalized user installation.
  c. graphical user interface.
  d. generated user interface.
  e. none of the above

7. Which of the following terms is used to refer to any window that appears on the screen for the purpose of communicating with the user?
  a. control window
  b. dialog box
  c. message box
  d. input window
  e. external window

8. Which of the following keyboard keys is commonly used in association with a letter or numeric key to create a shortcut key for a command or menu item?
  a. Esc
  b. Alt
  c. Tab
  d. Ctrl
  e. all of the above

9. If the Solution Explorer window is not visible when a project is opened, you can make it visible by selecting Solution Explorer from which menu?
  a. View
  b. Tools
  c. Window
  d. Project
  e. Edit

10. Which of the following menus contains commands that allow you to add files or components to an existing project?
  a. Edit
  b. Tools
  c. Build
  d. Format
  e. Project

11. Although its location can be changed, where is the Toolbox normally located when you create or open a Visual Basic project?
    a. It is at the top of the screen, below the Standard toolbar.
    b. It is on the right side of the screen.
    c. It is on the left side of the screen.
    d. It is at the bottom of the screen.
    e. It is usually invisible when a project starts, and must be turned on by the user.

12. The small black rectangles that appear around the border of a control when it is selected are called
    a. perimeter markers.
    b. sizing handles.
    c. relocation handles.
    d. boundary markers.
    e. adjustment sliders.

13. The Toolbox can be set to disappear when it is not being accessed by selecting which of the following features?
    a. Auto Hide
    b. Toolbox Hide
    c. Toolbox Invisible
    d. Hide Until Used
    e. Auto Vanish

14. Which option can be selected from the Toolbox's shortcut menu that allows you to add additional components or controls to the Toolbox?
    a. Add New
    b. Copy
    c. Customize Toolbox
    d. Add Control
    e. Add Component

15. Which property below can be modified to change the color of a control's background?
    a. Background Color
    b. Color
    c. Background Shade
    d. Back Color
    e. Back Shade

16. Which of the following is the recommended standard prefix to use when naming a file list box?
    a. lst
    b. fil
    c. flb
    d. fle
    e. lfb

17. The Properties window normally list the properties for an object in alphabetical order, with the exception of which property?
    a. Name
    b. Description
    c. Text
    d. Size
    e. Type

18. The Visual Basic area used to build the visual appearance of an application is called the
    a. Code window.
    b. Form area.

    c. Graphics area.

    d. Interface area.

    e. Designer area.

19. Which term is used to refer to a particular object created by a class?

    a. sibling

    b. child

    c. instantiation

    d. occurrence

    e. ancestor

20. What file extension is used to identify a Visual Basic solution file?

    a. .sol

    b. .slu

    c. .slt

    d. .sln

    e. none of the above

MATCHING

Write the letter of the description in the right column that defines the term in the left column.

_____ **1.** toolbar	**a.**	Additional tools that can be added to the Toolbox
_____ **2.** Toolbox	**b.**	Displays forms and modules in the project
_____ **3.** three-letter prefix	**c.**	Displays brief information about what the control does
_____ **4.** docking	**d.**	Property that every object has
_____ **5.** Pointer	**e.**	Attaching program tools to the IDE
_____ **6.** Solution Explorer window	**f.**	Displays tools for creating forms used in applications
_____ **7.** Properties window	**g.**	Characters in an object's name that identify its type
_____ **8.** components	**h.**	Displays and allows programmer to edit object properties
_____ **9.** ToolTip	**i.**	Displays buttons for frequently used functions
_____**10.** Name	**j.**	Tool used to select objects

FILL IN THE BLANK

Complete the following sentences by writing the correct word or words in the blanks provided.

1. Items found on the File menu of almost every Windows application include _____, _____, and _____.

2. The first general-purpose computer was named _____.

3. Examples of events include _____, _____, and _____.

4. Examples of objects that are used in Visual Basic programs include _____, _____, and _____.

5. A programmer must think about the _____ in which the user accesses the forms.

6. _____ are the main building blocks of a Visual Basic application.

7. A valid name in Visual Basic may not contain any _____ or _____.

8. The _____ property changes the text on a label.

9. The extension for the file containing the project components is _____.

10. A(n) _____ event occurs when the user clicks the mouse inside an application.

11. The _____ option within Help lets you look up all instances of a particular word or words within the documentation.

WRITTEN QUESTIONS

Write a brief answer to the following questions.

1. Why is the GUI aspect of Visual Basic so useful to programmers?

2. What are shortcut keys?

3. Why is Visual Basic such a popular programming language?

4. What does it mean for a program to be event driven?

5. What is the difference between colored buttons and dimmed buttons on the toolbar?

6. How can the Toolbox be moved to a different location on the IDE?

7. Why should you change the names of the objects added to a project from the default names assigned to them by Visual Basic?

8. What is an appropriate name for a text field that contains a person's birthday?

9. If the list of forms is not visible in your Solution Explorer window, and you want to see the forms contained in the project, what should you do?

10. Suppose your program has a form named *frmSurprise*. When you save that form, what will the file it is stored in be named?

11. Give three ways in which you can customize a label using the label properties.

12. Where are the Help files used by Visual Basic located?

13. What buttons are used to run and test a program in Visual Basic?

14. What is the name of the code that a programmer writes to respond to an event?

PROJECT 1-1

Start Visual Basic and create a new Visual Basic Windows Application project. Change the Text property of the form to **My Riddle**. Add a label containing the text **The Riddle Machine**. Add three command buttons with the captions **Riddle, Answer,** and **Exit**.

When the user clicks the Riddle button, the question of the riddle displays in a message box. When the user clicks the Answer button, the answer to the riddle displays in another message box. The Exit button ends the program.

In addition to making the program work correctly, edit the properties of your buttons, text, and main form so that you have an attractive user interface. Make sure to name your form and controls correctly. Indent the code for the messages and for the Exit button. Use any riddle of your choice that can be easily displayed in the message boxes. When you save the program, create a **My Riddle** folder, and use **MyRiddle** as the name for the form and the project.

PROJECT 1-2

Start Visual Basic and create a new Visual Basic Windows Application project. Change the Text property of the form to **Test Properties**. Add two labels, two text boxes, and a command button to the form. Name the text boxes **txtText1** and **txtText2**. Access the Text property for each form and clear the default text so the boxes do not display anything. Change the Text property of the first label to **Default Setting**, and the second label to **Modified Setting**. Change the Text property of the command button to **Enter**, and name the button **btnEnter**. Arrange the controls as shown in Figure 1-1, with **txtText1** under the Default Setting label, and **txtText2** under the Modified Setting label.

FIGURE 1-1

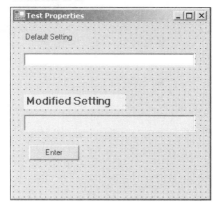

Click the **Modified Setting** label to select it, and click the **Font** property's ellipsis to open the Font dialog box. Change the font size to 12, and the font style to bold. Click the **Back Color** property, and select a light blue or light yellow color from the Custom color tab. Make the same font and color changes to the txtText2 text box located below the Modified Setting label.

Double-click the **Enter** button to open the Code window for the Click event procedure for that button. Enter the following code statements:

```
txtText1.Text = InputBox ("Please enter a short phrase")
txtText2.Text = txtText1.Text
```

Build and run the program. Click the **Enter** button. An input dialog box opens asking the user to enter a short phrase. Enter **My name is xxxx** where **xxxx** is your name. Click the **OK** button to close the dialog box. The phrase should then appear in both text boxes, although one is larger than the other. Experiment with other font sizes and color settings to see the results. When finished, save the project as **TestProperties** in the **TestProperties** folder.

PROGRAMMING AT WORK

This section begins a program that you will work on again in other Programming at Work sections in this workbook. It is designed to let you experience some of the challenges of creating larger, more meaningful programs.

Parents of school children need to make sure that before school begins in the fall, their children have the clothing and school supplies they need to start the year. Often parents have more than one child to prepare for school, and keeping track of who needs what and who has what is a challenging chore. In this project, you write a prototype of a program that could help parents keep track of this information for each of their children.

On the next page, design a program interface for keeping track of the information needed for a single child. Make sure to include the child's name, age, grade, and gender. The form has two lists: one for school supplies the student needs and one for clothing the student needs. Within each list, a parent can keep track of whether this child needs an item in the list, and if so, whether they have that item. You only need to think of four elements for each of your lists, as you are not developing a complete program. As you design the interface, think carefully about the tools you have available for building the GUI, and how you can use them to the best advantage. For example, in Lesson 2 you work with check boxes and option buttons. Check boxes are the most efficient way to check off as many items as needed from a list. Option buttons are used to give the user a single choice among items. Text boxes are where the user can key information. Think also about how to design a clear layout so that the information can be entered and read easily (including labels to describe other controls on the form).

WORKSHEET FOR PROGRAMMING AT WORK SOLUTION

Enter your program interface design on this page.

LESSON 2   FORMS AND DECISIONS

TRUE/FALSE

Circle T if the statement is true or F if the statement is false.

T   F   1. Each program you write should use completely different forms than any other program you have ever written.

T   F   2. The Exit button must have programming code written for it to work like it is supposed to.

T   F   3. You can access the Visual Basic Code window by clicking the Code button on the Standard toolbar.

T   F   4. You should only save a program after you have completely finished it.

T   F   5. The Height and Width properties of an object are measured in centimeters.

T   F   6. You can display a grid in the Designer to aid in the placement of controls by setting the ShowGrid property of the form to Visible.

T   F   7. The Look in list box allows the user to select which of the drives and folders on the computer should be accessed to locate a file.

T   F   8. A comment in the code is indicated by a leading double quote.

T   F   9. Check boxes and option buttons both allow you to choose multiple items at one time from a list of choices.

T   F   10. Copying a program is a perfectly acceptable way to obtain software inexpensively.

T   F   11. Complex logical expressions can be written using the connectors *And, But, Or,* and *Not.*

T   F   12. Relational operators cannot be used for expressions using strings.

MULTIPLE CHOICE

Select the best response for the following statements.

1. You should declare variables used in your program because
   a. Visual Basic requires it.
   b. doing so helps reduce errors due to misspellings.
   c. the program may function incorrectly if you do not.
   d. the author of the textbook recommends it.
   e. it makes the program shorter.

2. Which word indicates that you are declaring a variable?
   a. Var
   b. Variable
   c. Dim
   d. Declare
   e. DecVar

3. Which of the following is not a valid data type?
   a. Percent
   b. Long
   c. Byte
   d. Date
   e. String

4. Which data type is automatically assigned to a variable that is declared without a stated data type?
   a. Integer
   b. String
   c. Object
   d. Byte
   e. Boolean

5. Which of the following is the best name for an integer variable that holds the age of a pet?
   a. Age
   b. PetAge
   c. Pet Age
   d. intPetAge
   e. int Pet Age

6. What term is used to define the process of using an existing form for a new project and having access to all of its procedures and methods?
   a. reusability
   b. inheritance
   c. object relativity
   d. regeneration
   e. code incorporation

7. Which Visual Basic keyword is used to tell an application to stop processing?
   a. End
   b. EndApp
   c. AppEnd
   d. Stop
   e. Exit

8. Which property of a control can be modified to cause the control to maintain its same relative size and position if the form itself is resized?
   a. Size
   b. Location
   c. Position
   d. Anchor
   e. Scale

9. Which box at the top of the Code window can you access to select a different object to write code statements for?
   a. Method name
   b. Class name
   c. Object name
   d. Control name
   e. none of the above

10. Which form property must be set to True to make the grid visible?
    a. Grid
    b. ShowGrid
    c. DisplayGrid
    d. EnableGrid
    e. DrawGrid

11. What keyword can be used to refer to the current form when writing code statements?
    a. This
    b. Current

    c. Me

    d. My

    e. Last

12. Which property of the OpenFileDialog is used to determine the types of files to display in the file list?

    a. DefaultExt

    b. Filter

    c. InitialDirectory

    d. FileType

    e. List

13. Which Visual Basic feature anticipates what you are typing when entering code and offers suggestions as you type?

    a. IntelliSense

    b. CodeRecognition

    c. AnticiSense

    d. IntelliType

    e. none of the above

MATCHING

Write the letter of the description in the right column that defines the term in the left column.

_____ **1.** indentation	**a.** Terminates the application
_____ **2.** OK	**b.** The keyword used to declare a variable or constant
_____ **3.** Private Sub	**c.** Reference to the starting form (the currently running form)
_____ **4.** End	**d.** Places the starting form into memory and starts execution of a form on the screen
_____ **5.** Image	**e.** Property of the PictureBox control that opens a dialog box to locate the file for the PictureBox
_____ **6.** Class	**f.** One of the most common buttons in Windows programs
_____ **7.** Load	**g.** Removes the currently running form from memory and from the screen
_____ **8.** Close	**h.** A template used to create an object
_____ **9.** Me	**i.** Starts a routine that runs the code
_____ **10.** Dim	**j.** Makes the programming code more readable

FILL IN THE BLANK

Complete the following sentences by writing the correct word or words in the blanks provided.

1. The value of a(n) _____ can change while the program is running, but the value of a(n) _____ is the same throughout the program.

2. _____ a variable associates a name and a data type with the variable, and reserves a memory location for its use.

3. A Public variable is also referred to as a(n) _____ variable.

4. Variable declarations usually appear at the _____ of an event procedure.

5. Strings are contained in double quotes to distinguish them from _____.

6. When a variable is being assigned a value, the variable should always be on the _____ side of the equation.

7. The _____ of a variable describes the lifetime of the variable.

8. If you do not assign a data type when declaring a variable, Visual Basic automatically assigns the _____ data type to the variable.

9. A local variable is visible only in the _____ in which it is declared, a private variable is visible only in the _____ in which it is declared, and a public variable is visible in all _____.

10. The _____ of a variable determines the type of data it can store.

WRITTEN QUESTIONS

Write a brief answer to the following questions.

1. List three user-interface issues that the programmer should keep in mind while designing an application.

2. Explain why programming code is important for controls.

3. List the steps involved in creating a simple form.

4. What is the purpose of indentation when writing code, and does Visual Basic require you to use indentation?

5. What is a method?

6. What follows the *Sub* keyword in the Code window?

7. What properties affect the size and location of a form?

8. What control can be added to a form to allow a user to find and open a file located on a disk drive?

9. What control can be used to display a temporary dialog box containing text information to be displayed to the user?

10. What is the purpose of a PictureBox control, and what can it contain?

11. Why would you use constants in your programs instead of just using the actual numbers?

12. What are two differences between the Single data type and the Double data type?

13. What is good practice for choosing a variable name?

14. Write an appropriate variable name for an integer that stores someone's height.

15. Write a complete declaration of the variable described in question 14 for use in a single procedure.

16. What is the advantage of storing data as a variable rather than storing data in the property of an object?

17. Why would a programmer declare a public variable in the Declarations section of the code rather than declaring it within a procedure?

18. Write the complete declaration of a public string variable named strDoctor.

19. What is the Declarations section of a form used for? Why would you ever choose to define anything in the Declarations section?

20. Write a logical expression that is True whenever the variable dblBalance is not equal to zero and is not equal to 1000.

21. Write a logical expression that is True whenever the variable dblBalance is less than zero, or when it is greater than 10.

PROJECT 2-1

Create a form to open a file, similar to the project you designed in Step-by-Step 2.3 in the text. Follow the same procedure described in the text. Name the project **ConfirmFindFile** in a folder named **ConfirmFindFile**. Name your form **frmOpenFile2**, and change its Text property to **File Open Form**. Add a label to the form indicating that the form can be used to open a file. Add a button below the label named **btnOpen**, and change the Text property to **Open**. Add an **OpenFileDialog** control, and set up the code for that control as you did in Step-by-Step 2.3.

Below the Open button, add another label asking the user if they found their file. Below the label, add three buttons. Name one **btnYes** with a Text property of **Yes**. Name the second one **btnNo** with a text property of **No**. Name the third one **btnExit** with a Text property of **Exit**.

Add code so that when the Yes button is clicked, a message appears congratulating the user on finding their file, when the No button is clicked, a message appears sympathizing with the user, and when the Exit button is clicked, the application exits. Make sure you name your form and all controls appropriately. Also be sure to include indents and comments in your code.

PROJECT 2-2

In the blanks below, write a word of the specified type:

Name _____

Past-tense verb _____

Now replace the first blank in the sentence below with the Name, and the second with the verb:

_____ drank the soda and _____ around.

You have just created a Madlib! You can create another Madlib by substituting a different name and verb into the blanks above. The Madlib is generally a grammatically correct sentence, but be very silly instead of meaningful.

Write a program that creates a Madlib with the following structure:

The (animal) (verb) (preposition) the (noun).

Note that the items listed above in parentheses are declared in a standard module. The application has a label at the top with the caption **Madlib Mania** (your form uses the same caption). The form has three command buttons on it: **Create Madlib**, **Display Madlib**, and **Exit**.

Clicking on Create Madlib prompts the user to input an animal, verb, preposition, and a noun using successive input boxes. Clicking on Display Madlib displays the Madlib sentence in a message box. (The code for this is a string similar to the one you used in Step-by-Step 2.6. You need to experiment with spacing within your string.) Clicking on Exit terminates the program.

Use **Madlib** as the name for your form, module, and project (store the files in a folder called **Madlib**). Be sure to give each control within the program an appropriate name. In your code be sure to use indents and appropriate comments (don't forget the Option Explicit statement).

PROGRAMMING AT WORK

Implement the design plan you wrote for the school supplies and clothes needs in the Lesson 1 Programming at Work activity. If you did not include them in your plan, add an **Exit** command button and a **Reset** command button. Add the necessary code so that using the Exit button terminates the program. Also add code so that when the Reset button is clicked, the form is cleared of all entries. Here is an example of how to clear a text box named txtName, an option button named optFemale, and a check box named chkNeedShoes:

```
'Clear text box
txtName.Text = ""
'Clear option button
optFemale.Checked= False
'Clear check box
chkNeedShoes.Checked = False
```

Note: A check box control also has a CheckState property that can be used to reset it. Check the online Help system for information on the CheckState property and its usage.

If you used other controls for input, you need to look at the Property list for the control and determine what property is storing the value of the control. Then determine what value for that property makes the control empty, and use code similar to that shown above to clear the input from the control. You may have to do some trial-and-error work to determine the property and its value. Use **School** as the name for your form and project, and store your files in a folder named **School2**.

LESSON 3   MENUS, MDIs, AND SIMPLE LOOPS

TRUE/FALSE

Circle T if the statement is true or F if the statement is false.

T   F   **1.** The Help menu is usually the first menu listed on the menu bar.

T   F   **2.** Keying a pound (#) sign in front of a letter in the menu caption creates an access key for the menu item.

T   F   **3.** Separator bars are created in between menus on a menu bar to physically separate one menu from the menu on either side of it.

T   F   **4.** A shortcut for a menu item can be created from the MainMenu tool.

T   F   **5.** In the MainMenu tool, items within a menu are listed and indented under the menu to which they belong.

T   F   **6.** A dimmed item in a menu means that item is currently being used.

T   F   **7.** All menu controls recognize the Click event.

T   F   **8.** Menu bars are only rarely needed in a Windows application.

T   F   **9.** You should always list the menu items within a menu in alphabetical order.

T   F   **10.** Menu titles are listed on a menu bar, while submenu titles are listed within a menu.

T   F   **11.** Once you have positioned a menu item, its location cannot be changed using the MainMenu tool.

T   F   **12.** Separator bars are allowed in submenus as well as in menus.

T   F   **13.** The value of the control variable of a definite loop should be changed as the last statement within the loop code.

T   F   **14.** A definite loop can have a Step increment of any amount, including negative numbers.

T   F   **15.** Only constant values can be used as the start and end values for a definite loop.

T   F   **16.** The word "Step" must appear in every For statement.

MULTIPLE CHOICE

Select the best response for the following statements.

1. Which of the following cannot be done from the MainMenu tool?
   a. create a menu
   b. create a submenu
   c. preview a menu
   d. add a shortcut key to a menu item
   e. add an access key to a menu item

2. The menu item Save would logically belong in which menu?
   a. File
   b. Edit
   c. Window
   d. Operations
   e. Help

3. Which property of a menu item can be set to False to make the menu item appear dimmed and unavailable for selection?
   a. Visible
   b. ForeColor
   c. Usable
   d. Enabled

4. Which of the following is *not* a basic convention for Windows menus?
   a. putting the File and Edit menus first and the Help menu last on the menu bar
   b. starting all menu titles with a capital letter
   c. using short, specific captions
   d. starting the names of all menu items with the prefix "mnu"
   e. all of these are basic conventions for Windows menus

5. Which of the following events are recognized by a menu item?
   a. Click
   b. Change
   c. Enter key being pressed on the keyboard
   d. both a and c
   e. a, b, and c

6. Visual Basic supplies a color constant for which of the following colors?
   a. orange
   b. cyan
   c. purple
   d. brown
   e. chartreuse

7. How many color management systems does Visual Basic allow you to select from when you click the list arrow for the ForeColor property?
   a. one
   b. two
   c. three
   d. four
   e. more than four

8. The key that is used most often in a shortcut, along with a letter, is
   a. Alt
   b. Ctrl
   c. Esc
   d. F1
   e. Shift

MATCHING

Write the letter of the description in the right column that defines the term in the left column.

_____ 1. MDI

_____ 2. tile

_____ 3. MDIList

_____ 4. cascade

_____ 5. MDI form

_____ 6. Child form

_____ 7. MDIChild

_____ 8. Show

_____ 9. Window

_____ 10. LayoutMDI

a. A property used to indicate a form is a child of an MDI parent

b. Form that contains all the other forms in an MDI

c. A method that can be invoked to change the way forms are displayed

d. The menu you can click to display a list of all open documents in an application

e. Application that contains multiple windows within another window

f. Code that opens an existing form

g. Form contained within and directly linked to the main MDI application

h. A menu item property that when set to True uses that menu item to list all child forms in the application

i. Option for arranging windows on top or beside each other

j. A means of displaying multiple forms by making them all the same size and slightly offsetting each one to the right and below the previous form

FILL IN THE BLANK

Complete the following sentences by writing the correct word or words in the blanks provided.

1. The MDI allows you to create an application that has _____ forms that are contained within one _____ form.

2. The forms that make up an MDI application have a(n) _____ and _____ relationship.

3. In an MDI with four child forms, there would be _____ main menu(s).

4. The term MDI is an acronym for _____.

5. The _____ menu in an MDI application usually contains a list of the open windows and options for arranging the display of multiple windows.

6. A form can be made invisible to the user without unloading the form from memory by calling the _____ method.

7. Many MDI applications contain a(n) _____ form, which is used to provide information about the company, the program, the version of the program, and possibly copyright information as well.

8. If a For loop is to cycle through an array from the end to the beginning, the Step increment must be _____.

WRITTEN QUESTIONS

Write a brief answer to the following questions.

1. State two of the basic elements of a menu.

2. How do you make the MainMenu tool appear?

3. How do you create a separator bar within a menu?

4. Suppose you are creating a menu named Pets. Within that menu are two submenus, Cats and Dogs. The submenu Cats contains the items Domestic Short Haired and Domestic Long Haired, while the Dogs submenu contains the items Purebred and Mixed Breed. Draw what this series of menu items would look like when using the MainMenu tool to create the menu.

5. For the menu you drew in question 4, what would be the name you should use for the item Cats? How about for the item Purebred?

6. Why should a programmer not use too many levels of submenus in a program?

7. Describe two differences between access keys and shortcut keys for menu items.

8. In which menu do users of Windows programs expect to find the About box?

9. Suppose you are writing a program that uses the menu in question 4. The application has two text boxes, one named txtAnimal and one named txtAnimalBreed. Write a code fragment that shows what should be done to put the type of animal and its breed into their respective text boxes when the user clicks on Mixed Breed. (*Note*: this is similar to what you did in Step-by-Step 3.4, except that you must modify the Text property of the text box instead of the ForeColor item. You also need to use quotation marks for your strings.)

10. Write another line of code that puts a check mark by the menu item Mixed Breed when it is selected. (Do not worry about deselecting any other menu items.)

11. Give an example of an MDI application you are familiar with other than Microsoft Word.

12. In an MDI application, which form is referred to as the parent? Which are referred to as the children?

13. What must be done in the child forms to get them to open within the MDI form?

14. How do you specify that a form is to be an MDI parent form?

15. Write the line of code that would be used to create a child form from a template form named myChild.

16. Draw a picture that shows what three cascaded windows in an MDI look like. Label the main window Main Window and the other three windows Window 1, Window 2, and Window 3.

17. Draw a picture that shows what three windows in an MDI look like if they are tiled horizontally. Label the main window Main Window and the other three windows Window 1, Window 2, and Window 3.

18. Draw a picture that shows what three windows in an MDI look like if they are tiled vertically. Label the main window Main Window and the other three windows Window 1, Window 2, and Window 3.

19. Assuming a template form is being used to create child forms, and the template form contains a menu, what steps are involved in adding the menu to the parent form menu when a new child is created during program execution?

20. Think of another form you might make that would be reusable in many applications you will write.

21. Write a definite loop that prints out the numbers 10, 9, 8, ..., 1 using a message box to display each value.

22. Suppose you have an array variable strBooks that has a list of 100 book titles in it. Describe the algorithm for performing a linear search on this array to check if a book title that the user enters is in the array.

PROJECT 3-1

Create a simple drawing program with three menus in the menu bar: **File**, **Shapes**, and **Tools**. Within the File menu are the options **Open**, **Save**, **Print**, and **Exit**. Two separator bars are used in this menu, one after Save and one after Print. The Shapes menu allows the user to select a **Circle**, **Rectangle**, or **Triangle**. The Tools menu contains a **Drawing** submenu and a **Painting** submenu. The Drawing submenu gives the user the options to use a **Pen** or **Chalk**, and the Painting submenu lets the user choose between **Brush** and **Bucket**.

Provide an access key for each menu name and each of the items in the menus. Provide a shortcut key for each of the shapes and each of the drawing and painting tools. Add a label containing the words **Item Selected** and a text box below the label. Initially, the text box is empty.

The menu item Exit terminates the program when selected. When an item is selected in the Drawing or Painting submenu, a check mark is added to the item. For every menu item but Exit, when the item is selected, the program writes the text of the selected item into the text box. For example, if the text box name is txtItemSelected, then the way to implement this for the Open item of the File menu is to add the following code to the function

```
mnuFileOpen_Click():
    txtItemSelected.Text = "Open"
```

Save the program using **DrawMenu** as the name for the form and project in a folder named **DrawMenu**. Be sure to follow the naming conventions described in the text as you write the program. In your code use indents and appropriate comments.

PROJECT 3-2

The simple drawing program of the previous section can also be implemented using an MDI. In this implementation, the application has two child windows, one for the tools and one for the drawing palette. The main application contains only the menu bar with three menus: **File**, which contains the options **Open**, **Save**, **Print**, and **Exit** and the two separators as before; **View**, which contains the options **Tools** and **Palette**; and **Window**, which allows the user to change the display of the windows and includes the **WindowList** feature. Each menu name and each of the items in the menus has an access key associated with it.

The child form with the drawing palette has the caption **Palette**. The palette contains a label plus the text box into which the names of selected items are written as in the previous application.

The second child form has the caption **Tools**. This form has a long and narrow toolbox with the options that used to be under the Shapes and Tools menus (**Circle**, **Rectangle**, **Triangle**, **Pen**, **Chalk**, **Brush**, and **Bucket**). One way to design the toolbox is to put seven labels on the form, each with a word describing what it does. When the user clicks a label, the text associated with the label that was clicked is written to the text box in the drawing palette.

You need to access the Palette form from the Tools form. One way to do this is to create a module for the project, and declare the Palette and the Tools forms in that module as global variables. For example, in the Declarations section of the module define the Palette form using a statement such as the following:

```
Public NewPalette As New frmPalette
```

Now, any class or procedure within the project can access the NewPalette form. In the main form code, when the user clicks the Palette option on the View menu, you would display the form by using the following statement in the Click Procedure for the Palette menu option:

```
NewPalette.Show()
```

The Tools form code can also access the globally defined form when one of the labels is clicked by using the following statement in the proper Click event procedure:

```
NewPalette.txtSelected.Text = "xxxxx" , where xxxxx is the label selected
(Circle, Pen, etc.)
```

Create a new project named **DrawMDI**, which implements the application described above. Note that the Open, Save, and Print menu options are not functional, but all the others perform their appropriate function. When you run your program, test all items. To test the text box, you may find it helpful to cascade the Tools and Palette forms. Name your two child forms **frmTools** and **frmPalette**. As always, name controls in the conventional manner, and be sure to include indents and appropriate comments in your code. Save all your work in a folder named **DrawMDI**.

PROGRAMMING AT WORK

Rewrite the school supplies and clothes needs program that you created in the Lesson 2 Programming at Work exercise so that you have an MDI application. The application has three child forms: one for the child's information, one for the clothing list, and one for the supply list. Incorporate an About form as an additional child form to be accessed from the main form. On the parent form is a **File** menu that has the items **Reset** and **Exit**. These menu items work like the Reset and Exit buttons did in the Lesson 2 Programming at Work exercise (you can delete the buttons). Note that in Reset, you have to put the form name for the item that is to be cleared and a dot before each of the names of the controls. (For example: frmInfo.txtAge.Text = ""). An **Open** menu on the parent form opens each of the three child windows. A **Window** menu on the parent form functions like the Window menu you developed in the text Step-by-Step exercises and in Project 3-2. Finally, a **Help** menu on the parent form provides access to the About form. Each of the menu items has an access key.

As always, be careful and consistent in your naming of the forms and controls as you create them. Be sure to include indents and appropriate comments in your code. By now, you know to make sure your forms and controls have appropriate names, and to indent and comment appropriately. You will no longer be reminded to do this, but are still expected to do so for every programming exercise.

As in the previous MDI activity in this lesson, you need to add a module to the program and you declare the Info, Clothes, and Supplies forms in the module as Public variables so any form can be accessed from any other form. Use the skills you learned in the previous MDI application to create this application. Save the project as **MDISchool** in a folder named **MDISchool**.

Run the application and test it. Be sure that when the Reset option is clicked on the main form that all fields are cleared on all child forms. Tile the windows horizontally and vertically. Are all fields on all forms visible? If not, try dragging the borders between the forms to see if you can make all fields on all forms visible at the same time.

LESSON 4   DECISIONS, LOOPING, ARRAYS, AND SEARCHING
TRUE/FALSE

Circle T if the statement is true or F if the statement is false.

T   F   1. When designing and writing an application for users, you may need to speak with them several times to make sure the program meets their needs.

T   F   2. Once you have developed an algorithm to solve the problem, you are ready to start writing the code.

T   F   3. Trade-offs to consider when choosing a data structure for solving a problem are how much time it will take to access information versus how much memory space will be required.

T   F   4. When an application uses a combo box, the user cannot enter any text directly into the text area, but must select one of the entries in the list.

T   F   5. An array is a list of values referred to by a single variable name.

T   F   6. Code that executes before the form is displayed, such as initializing a list box, should be put in the Class section of the form.

T   F   7. Any If statement used in a program must be terminated by the End If statement.

T   F   8. Every Select Case statement must have a Case Else component.

T   F   9. An indefinite loop always terminates eventually.

T   F   10. The lowest value of any array index is always zero.

T   F   11. A linear search is the best way to find an element in an unordered list.

T   F   12. An indefinite loop is most useful when you know exactly how many times you need to execute the code inside the loop.

T   F   13. An array is a list of values with the same name, the individual elements of which are distinguished from one another by their unique index values.

T   F   14. The term "flag" is used for a variable that is used as an indicator that something has happened in the program.

T   F   15. The step-by-step solution to a problem is called an algorithm.

T   F   16. A list box is typically used to enter data from a user, while a combo box is normally used to display lists of data for the user.

T   F   17. Enclosing one or more If statements inside another If statement is called statement embedding.

T   F   18. The Do Until loop structure always executes the code statements in the body of the loop at least once, and the loop continues to execute as long as the control condition is false.

MATCHING

Write the letter of the description in the right column that defines the term in the left column.

_____ 1. user interface

_____ 2. algorithm

_____ 3. stepwise refinement

_____ 4. event procedure

_____ 5. combo box

_____ 6. list box

_____ 7. program flow

_____ 8. collection

_____ 9. sentinel

_____ 10. array

_____ 11. &

_____ 12. Abs

_____ 13. Rint

_____ 14. Floor

_____ 15. Ucase

_____ 16. InStr

_____ 17. InStrRev

_____ 18. Trim

_____ 19. Len

_____ 20. Lcase

_____ 21. Mid

_____ 22. Val

_____ 23. StrReverse

_____ 24. Str

a. Subroutine associated with a button or text box

b. A text box with an attached list displaying only a single item

c. The sequence in which the code statements are executed

d. A list of values referred to by a single name

e. An object that contains other related objects

f. How the user interacts with the program

g. A value input from a keyboard or data file that terminates loop processing

h. Step-by-step solution to a program

i. Displays a list showing all or several of the items

j. Breaking a problem into small subproblems, each of which is fairly easy to solve

k. Rounds to the next lower integer

l. Returns the number of characters in a string

m. Converts a value to a string representation

n. Computes the absolute value of a number

o. Removes any leading or trailing spaces from a string

p. Converts a string to all lowercase letters

q. Converts a string to all uppercase letters

r. Rounds to the nearest integer

s. Returns a string whose characters are in reverse order from the input string

t. Concatenation operator for strings

u. Computes the start position of one string embedded in another

v. Returns the substring of a string, starting at a specified position and containing a specified number of characters

w. Converts a string to a value

x. Computes the start position of one string embedded in another, but starting from the back of the string and working from right to left

FILL IN THE BLANK

Complete the following sentences by writing the correct word or words in the blanks provided.

1. The _____ of a loop contains the code to be executed each time through the loop.

2. The _____ method removes the contents of a list box.

3. The value of 14 Mod 5 is _____.

4. The loop structure that repeats until a condition becomes True is the _____.

5. If an array is declared Dim strWords(12) As String, the lowest index value is _____, while the highest index value is _____.

6. A variable declared within a procedure is a(n) _____ variable.

7. The _____ of a variable is when it does and does not hold valid values.

8. The _____ of a variable is where in the project the value of the variable is available to use or change.

WRITTEN QUESTIONS

Write a brief answer to the following questions.

1. What is a subroutine?

2. What is a data structure? Give an example of a data structure.

3. Why does writing the code come so late in the process of solving a problem with a computer program?

4. Write a one-line If statement that puts the value "Excellent" into the variable txtResult.Text if the value of the variable intScore is greater than or equal to 90.

5. Write an If statement that puts the value "Excellent" into the variable txtResult.Text if the value of the variable intScore is greater than or equal to 90 using a multiple-line version of the If statement you wrote in the previous question.

6. Write an If-Else statement that puts the value "Excellent" into the variable txtResult.Text if the value of the variable intScore is greater than or equal to 90, and puts in the value "OK" otherwise.

7. Write an If-ElseIf statement that puts the value "Excellent" into the variable txtResult.Text if the value of the variable intScore is greater than or equal to 90, "Good" if intScore is less than 90 but greater than or equal to 80, "Satisfactory" if intScore is less than 80 but greater than or equal to 70, "Poor" if intScore is less than 70 but greater than or equal to 60, and "Unsatisfactory" if intScore is less than 60.

8. Write an If-ElseIf statement that puts the value "lowercase" into the variable txtLetterCase.Text if the character contained in the variable intChar is a lowercase letter, "uppercase" if intChar is an uppercase letter, and "Not a Letter" if intChar is neither an uppercase nor a lowercase letter.

9. What is the difference between a definite loop and an indefinite loop?

10. Describe the actions that occur as the following code executes:

```
intX = 8
Do Until intX < 5
    intX = intX - 2
Loop
```

11. What is the value of X after each code fragment below finishes executing?

Code 1:	**Code 2:**	**Code 3:**
intX = 4	intX = 4	intX = 4
Do	Do While intX > 5	Do While intX < 5
intX = intX - 2	intX = intX - 2	intX = intX - 2
Loop While intX > 5	Loop	Loop

12. How many times does the following loop execute?

```
For intX = 0 to 7 Step 0.2
    intY = intY + intX
Next intX
```

13. Write a declaration of an array of integers named intNumbers with 20 elements in it.

14. How can you determine if one number is evenly divisible by some other number?

15. Suppose that values have been put into the array you declared in question 5. Write a code fragment that displays a message telling whether or not the number 5 occurs within the array.

16. Write the code required to declare an array named dblArray with a data type of Double, and that also initializes the first three array entries to the following values:

    index(0) = 10496.85
    index(1) = 982.76
    index(2) = 12.48

17. Write a code fragment to compute the distance between two points (Xl, Yl) and (X2, Y2). The distance between two points is given by the formula

$$\sqrt{(X2 - X1)^2 + (Y2 - Y1)^2}$$

    Use variable names dblXl, dblY1, dblX2, dblY2, and dblDistance in your code.

18. Write a code fragment to decide whether the difference in x coordinates of two points is greater than the difference between the y coordinates and display a message box telling which is bigger, or a message box that both are equal. For two points (xl, yl) and (x2, y2), you need to compare the absolute values [x2-xl] and [y2-yl].

19. Suppose you have an angle in degrees stored in the variable dblAngle. Write a code fragment that first converts the angle to its measure in radians, and then computes the sine of the angle and puts the value into the variable dblSine.

20. What function should you use if you need to raise a number to some specified power?

21. What function should you use if you need to determine the square root of a number?

22. What function would you use to obtain a random number greater than or equal to zero, but less than one?

23. Suppose you have a string variable named strNumber and a double variable named dblNumber. Write a code fragment that assigns dblNumber the value represented by the string in strNumber.

24. Suppose you have a string variable named strPhrase. Write a code fragment to decide if the string "and" is contained in strPhrase, and display a message box with the location if it was found, or a message that it was not in strPhrase if it was not found. (*Hint:* The function InStr returns zero if it does not find str2 inside strl.)

25. Suppose you have a string variable named strPhrase, and you want to decide if it is a palindrome or not. Write a code fragment that converts the case and checks to see if the phrase is the same backwards and forwards, then displays a message box stating the phrase and whether it is a palindrome or not. Recall that a palindrome is a phrase that reads the same backwards and forwards, ignoring capitalization and punctuation. You may assume there is no punctuation in the phrase.

26. Suppose you have a string variable named strPhrase, and you want to remove the first occurrence of the character "x" from the phrase, if there is an "x" in the phrase. Otherwise the phrase should remain the same. Write a code fragment that performs this task.

PROJECT 4-1

Write a program that implements the problem described in Written Question 7, but uses a Select Case statement instead of an If-ElseIf statement to make the decision about what to put in txtResult.Text. In particular, the user interface contains two text boxes, one for the score and one for the result. The Text properties are initially blank for the text boxes. Each text box has a corresponding label. The GUI displays two command buttons: **Go** and **Exit**, each of which has an access key. The code for the Go button first converts the value of the Score text box into an integer and stores the value in a variable named intScore. The code to do this is:

```
intScore = Val (txtScore.Text)
```

The next step is to clear the Result text box. Finally, use the variable intScore in the Select Case statement to decide what to put into the result text box. (*Hint:* use a range.)

Name your form and project **TestCase**, and save them in a folder named **TestCase**.

PROJECT 4-2

Two things that are often of interest about a list is what position in the array contains the first occurrence of a particular value, and how many times a particular value appears in the array. The linear search program in Step-by-Step 4.4 of the student text reports the first occurrence of a value in an array, if there is one. In this program, you count the number of occurrences of a value in an array. You create an array of 20 randomly chosen numbers the values of which are all in the range zero to five, inclusive. The user is able to enter a value between zero and five, and then ask the program to count how many times the value appears in the array.

Create a GUI with a long narrow list box on the left and five command buttons. The button captions are **Instructions**, **Generate List**, **Get Number**, **Count Occurrences**, and **Exit**.

The Instructions button displays a message box with directions for using the program. The code is

```
MessageBox.Show ( "Click Generate List to begin. " & vbCr & vbLf & _
"Click Get Number, input a number, and click OK." & vbCr & vbLf & _
"Click Count Occurrences to count how many times your number appears in the
list." & vbCr & vbLf & _
"Click Get Number to count another number from the same list." & vbCr & vbLf
 & _
"Click Generate List to get a new list.")
```

The code & vbCr & vbLf adds a carriage return to the message box text. The underscore allows the code to continue onto another line. Do not press Enter in the middle of a message; end your lines where the underscores appear in this code.

Each time the user clicks Generate List, the program first clears the list box, and then creates a new list of 20 random numbers between zero and five. Suppose you have named your array that holds the data int Numbers. The code to put a random number between zero and five into position intX of intNumbers is:

```
IntNumbers (intX) = Rnd ( ) *5
```

In order to get a different sequence of numbers each time you run the program, the following line of code must be put into the form's Activate subroutine:

```
Randomize
```

When the user clicks Get Number, an Input Box prompts the user to input a number between zero and five, inclusive. Use a loop that continues to prompt for a number until the user enters a number that is within the valid range. When the user clicks Count Occurrences, the program searches the entire list to count the number of occurrences of the selected number. To implement this, declare an integer variable intCounter. Initialize it to zero immediately before the loop that cycles through the array. Within the loop, check if the current array value is equal to the selected number. Every time the two are equal, increase intCounter by 1. Display a message after the search is completed telling how many times the value occurred (even if it is zero times). The Exit button terminates the application.

Save your form and project as **ListCounter** in a folder named **ListCounter**.

PROJECT 4-3

Write a program that computes the two roots of a quadratic equation $ax^2 + bx + c = 0$. The roots of the equation $ax^2 + bx + c = 0$ are:

Root 1 =

$$\frac{-b + \sqrt{b^2 - 4ac}}{2a}$$

Root 2 =

$$\frac{-b - \sqrt{b^2 - 4ac}}{2a}$$

The GUI for the application contains three text boxes for the user to enter input, and two to display the roots. The three input text boxes have associated labels with the captions A, B, and C, while the two display text boxes have associated labels with the captions Root 1 and Root 2. A Go button on the user interface gets the values from the input text boxes and uses them to compute the roots. In the Go button's Click event, first compute the discriminant, $b^2 - 4ac$. If its value is less than zero, there are no real roots, and a message box lets the user know this fact. If its value is greater than or equal to zero, compute the two roots and display them in the appropriate text boxes on the screen. (*Hint*: The function Str converts the double value of a root to a string data type, so that the value can be put into the text box.) A Clear button on the GUI resets all the text boxes to blanks, and an Exit button allows the user to exit the program.

To test your program, first try values of 1 for A, 3 for B, and 2 for C. Then clear the screen and try other values.

Save your form and project as **Quadratic** in a folder named **Quadratic**.

PROGRAMMING AT WORK

This project involves creating a system for a medical office to keep track of information about their patients. The complete project will be developed over many of the remaining Programming at Work activities in this workbook. Your final project will be a tool with features that would be expected in a realistic implementation of such a product.

In this beginning stage of the project, you develop an interface for entering patient data. The data needed for each patient is their:

Id Number
Last Name
First Name
Street Address
City, State, and ZIP Code
Phone Number
Primary Physician
Insurance Provider

The **Primary Physician** and **Insurance Provider** fields are combo boxes. There are at least four physicians in the practice; you may make up names for them! The last option for the Primary Physician combo box is **Other (Enter Name)** to handle cases where the patient is not a regular patient at this office. Include at least two insurance providers in the Insurance Provider combo box, and an option to enter a provider not listed in your list. The other input fields are text boxes. Use the order shown above as the order of the entry fields on your form. (*Note*: Use the With shortcut to add items to your combo boxes.)

There are three command buttons at the bottom of the form: **Record**, **Clear**, and **Exit**. Make sure that each button has an access key associated with it. The Record button is used in later lessons to add an entry to the system. The Clear button resets all entries to an empty state. The Exit button, of course, terminates the program. For this part of the project, you need only enter code for the Clear and Exit buttons. Verify that the data entry and Clear and Exit buttons work as you planned.

Name the form **frmPatientInfoEntry**, and give it the caption **Patient Information Entry**. Save your form as **PatientInfoEntry** and your project as **MedicalRecords** in a folder named **MedicalRecordsl**.

UNIT 1   REVIEW

TRUE/FALSE

Circle T if the statement is true or F if the statement is false.

T   F   **1.** The informational box that sometimes appears when the mouse pointer is positioned over a control or toolbar button is called a QuickTip.

T   F   **2.** Every user on any Visual Studio .NET system always sees the same startup page when the program is started.

T   F   **3.** The tools on the Visual Basic toolbars and in the Toolbox may vary from installation to installation due to different system configurations.

T   F   **4.** If the Toolbox is not visible when you start an application, you can display it by selecting the Toolbox option from the Tools menu.

T   F   **5.** The only way to rename a form is to access the *(Name)* property in the Properties window.

T   F   **6.** Modular programming languages allow a programmer to break problems into a series of smaller problems, each of which can then be solved individually.

T   F   **7.** Visual Basic automatically capitalizes keywords when entering code statements, and if it does not, you may have misspelled the word.

T   F   **8.** You can move multiple controls on a form at the same time by selecting all controls to be moved, and then dragging them to the new location.

T   F   **9.** A check box control is a round selection button that is part of a group, only one of which may be selected at a time.

T   F   **10.** Variables are defined using the Dim statement, and constants are defined using the DimC statement.

T   F   **11.** When planning a menu or an application, you need to consider which commands and options the users need, and in which order the commands and options should appear.

T   F   **12.** A check mark appears in front of a menu item if the item's Checked property is set to Visible.

T   F   **13.** You can assign a shortcut key to a menu item by selecting the item, and then accessing the Shortcut property in the Properties window.

T   F   **14.** When a new form is created in an MDI application, the program must call the Display method to make the form visible.

T   F   **15.** Creating the user interface is one of the last steps you would perform when building a new application program.

T   F   **16.** The entries displayed in a list box are called items, and all of the items taken together form the Items collection.

T   F   **17.** Do-While loops can be structured so that the body of the loop always executes at least once, no matter what the original value of the control condition is.

T   F   **18.** A Do-Until condition type of loop executes as long as the stated condition remains True.

T   F   **19.** When you do not know how many repetitions are required for a loop to finish processing, a For loop structure is the best loop to use.

T   F   **20.** Array subscripts can start with any value. For example, an array of 20 items could be specified to start with subscript 5 and end with subscript 24.

MULTIPLE CHOICE

Select the best response for the following statements.

1. Which of the following options is normally found on the File menu of a Windows application program?
   a. Copy
   b. Save
   c. Paste
   d. Quit
   e. both b and d

2. The collection of project(s) files that make up a Visual Basic application program is called a(n)
   a. package.
   b. project group.
   c. component.
   d. solution.
   e. cluster.

3. When designing a new application program, the best way to determine how the user wants the application to work is to
   a. carefully study the design specification for the application.
   b. talk to the user(s) who requested the application.
   c. visualize how you would want it to work.
   d. ask your supervisor for his/her opinions.
   e. all of the above

4. One way to open the Code window is to right-click the mouse in the Solution Explorer window, and then select which option from the shortcut menu?
   a. View Code
   b. Open Code Window
   c. Code
   d. Code Window
   e. Enter Code

5. Which of the following prefixes is the generally accepted naming convention for a 3-D command button?
   a. bt3
   b. btn
   c. cmd
   d. c3D
   e. cm3

6. A(n) _____ is any code routine included as part of a class definition of a form.
   a. macro
   b. object
   c. method
   d. event procedure
   e. none of the above

7. What are the two subproperties of a form's Location property?
   a. Height and Width
   b. xpos and ypos
   c. Left and Top
   d. X and Y
   e. FromLeft and FromTop

8. What does a Visual Basic program use to set and modify properties of a Visual Basic object?
   a. property controls
   b. property dialogs
   c. event modifiers
   d. method macros
   e. assignment statements

9. Which of the following alignment options can be specified when aligning multiple controls, such as radio buttons or labels, or text boxes?
   a. Align Tops
   b. Align Lefts
   c. Align Bottoms
   d. both a and b
   e. all of the above

10. Variables declared with which keyword can only be accessed within the module or procedure where they are defined?
    a. Private
    b. Local
    c. Restricted
    d. Limited
    e. none of the above

11. Which Visual Basic tool is used to create and edit menus?
    a. MenuWizard
    b. MenuList
    c. MainMenu
    d. Menu
    e. MenuTool

12. Which character is used to create a separator bar when creating a menu?
    a. dash (-)
    b. ampersand (&)
    c. equal sign (=)
    d. vertical bar (|)
    e. asterisk (*)

13. Which term is used to refer to the process of displaying multiple forms edge-to-edge so that they fill the window vertically or horizontally?
   a. cascade
   b. shrink-to-fit
   c. fit-to-window
   d. tile
   e. plaster

14. The body of a For loop should never
   a. use a Step increment of more than one.
   b. modify the control variable.
   c. contain an If statement.
   d. both a and b
   e. all of the above

15. Which of the following Visual Basic controls resembles a text box but presents the user with a list of items from which they can choose?
   a. compound box
   b. itemlist box
   c. combo box
   d. command box
   e. selection box

16. Which keyword is used to end a multi-line IfElse statement?
   a. End If
   b. End
   c. If End
   d. End If Else
   e. End Else

17. What is the purpose of the Visual Basic Mod operator?
   a. It is used to set the display mode for a form.
   b. It changes a True property to False and vice versa.
   c. It is used to modify some property of the currently selected object.
   d. It determines if there is a remainder value for a divide operation.
   e. none of the above

18. To make an array or other variable visible to all event procedures, where should it be declared in the Visual Basic code?
   a. in the Class section
   b. in the All Events section
   c. in the Load procedure
   d. in the Global section
   e. in the Declarations section

19. Which of the following examples of a For loop shows the correct syntax for the loop?
   a. For $x = 1$ To 100 Increment 2
   b. For $x = 1$ To 100 Step 1
   c. For $x = 1$ To 100
   d. For $x = 1$ To 100 By 1
   e. both b and c

20. Individual items in an array structure are commonly referred to as elements, and are also sometimes called which of the following?
   a. members
   b. units
   c. cells
   d. slots
   e. children

FILL IN THE BLANK

Complete the following sentences by writing the correct word or words in the blanks provided.

   1. A variety of prebuilt components, such as buttons and labels, can be added to a form by accessing them from the Visual Basic _____.

   2. Visual Basic _____ are the controls that make up a Visual Basic program.

   3. The window that lists all the forms and modules used in a particular project is the _____.

   4. In order to select objects on your form, you must use the _____ tool.

   5. Selecting the _____ tab of the Properties window allows you to view the properties grouped by such things as Appearance, Behavior, Data, and other groupings.

   6. Although it is not required, the practice of using _____ when writing code statements makes the code easier to read and to follow.

   7. _____ is the term used to define the set of rules every programming language uses to build and write program instructions.

   8. Everything in Visual Basic is an object, which is created from a(n) _____.

   9. The _____ property of the OpenFileDialog control is used to set the default file extension type.

   10. Visual Basic's _____ data type is used to define variables or constants that can only contain a value of True or False.

   11. _____ bars are thin lines that are used in menus to group related menu options.

   12. To access a menu item or command button via an access key, you must hold down the _____ key while pressing the letter or number underlined in the item.

   13. When the _____ property for a menu item is set to True, the property automatically uses that menu item to list all child forms in the application.

   14. The starting value, the upper limit, and the number of repetitions are all generally known in advance for a(n) _____ loop structure.

   15. Data _____ can be used to organize data according to the relationships that exist between the individual data items.

16. The condition represented by an If statement is called a(n) _____ expression, which results in a True or False condition when it is evaluated.

17. A(n) _____ value is a special value that can be input from a keyboard at the end of a file to indicate when a loop should stop processing.

18. The _____ of a variable determines when it can and cannot hold valid values.

19. In a For loop structure, the _____ operator is an optional parameter and the loop automatically increments by 1 if it is omitted.

20. Array elements are referenced by a subscript value, which is also commonly referred to as a(n) _____ value.

UNIT 2: COLLECTIONS

LESSON 5   **IMPROVING THE USER INTERFACE**

LESSON 6   **DATABASE PROGRAMMING**

LESSON 7   **DEBUGGING AND SIMPLE CLASSES**

LESSON 8   **CLASSES AND OBJECTS**

LESSON 9   **EXPLORING ALL KINDS OF COLLECTIONS**

UNIT 2 REVIEW

LESSON 5:   IMPROVING THE USER INTERFACE

TRUE/FALSE

Circle T if the statement is true or F if the statement is false.

T   F   1. The MessageBox control's default form shows a message to be displayed, an OK button, and a Cancel button.

T   F   2. If the user clicks the OK button in a message box, a string value of *Yes* is returned to the program.

T   F   3. The Icon property of the MessageBox control can be set with an argument that indicates what type of icon should display with the message.

T   F   4. When entering items for a combo box, you enter the items as part of the Items collection property.

T   F   5. The InputBox function returns only string data.

T   F   6. The InputBox function is always displayed in the center of the active form for the application.

T   F   7. A run-time error could occur from a user entering numeric data into a text box designed to hold character data.

T   F   8. A Visual Basic application may have multiple context menus defined, each one associated with a different control.

T   F   9. Once defined, a context menu cannot be modified while the application program is executing.

T   F   10. When building a toolbar, the first step is to attach an image list to the toolbar.

T   F   11. The ButtonSize property of the toolbar object contains a value of the Size data type, which determines the toolbar buttons dimensions.

T   F   12. Toolbars can be added to a form by double-clicking the Toolbar tool in the Visual Basic Toolbox.

T   F   13. The recommended prefix for naming an image list control is *ilc*.

T   F   14. Anytime a user initiates an event in an application, the event handler passes messages called parameters to the code in the event handler, and the parameters identify the event and the object initiating the event.

T   F   15. Visual Basic's RichTextBox control has characteristics more like those of a word processor than the standard TextBox control.

T   F   16. In addition to the controls available in the Toolbox, you can find additional controls on the Internet that have been created by other users, all of which are free for the taking.

T   F   17. When data is read from a text data file, each character in the file must be converted from binary format to character format.

T   F   18. When done reading data from a file, the Close method of the File object is called to close the data file.

T   F   19. The CreateText method of the File object is called to create a new text file.

T   F   20. To write text data to an output file, you must first create an OutputWriter object.

MULTIPLE CHOICE

Select the best response for the following statements.

1. The MessageBox is a(n) _____ dialog box, which means the user must respond to the message before processing can proceed.
   a. frozen
   b. ActiveX
   c. stand-alone
   d. modal
   e. static

2. Which MessageBox function button property below would you specify to display a message box with the OK and Cancel buttons included in the dialog box?
   a. MessageBox.OKCancel
   b. MessageBox.Buttons.OK.Cancel
   c. MessageBoxButtons.OK.Cancel
   d. MessageButton.OKCancel
   e. MessageBoxButtons.OKCancel

3. Which of the following properties is *not* a valid name for the Icon property of the MessageBox control?
   a. Error
   b. Fatal
   c. Hand
   d. Information
   e. Warning

4. Which character below, when preceded by a space, is used as a line continuation character in Visual Basic?
   a. ampersand (&)
   b. dash (-)
   c. underscore (_)
   d. asterisk (*)
   e. at sign (@)

5. What is returned to the program if a user clicks a Cancel button in an input box dialog box?
   a. 0 (zero)
   b. a null string
   c. -1 (minus 1)
   d. 1 (one)
   e. 2 (two)

6. What typically occurs when a program cannot perform a task that it expects to carry out?
   a. run-time error
   b. catastrophic crash
   c. program suspension
   d. program reset
   e. all of the above

7. What action below typically causes a context menu to pop up in an application?
   a. double-click a control
   b. press the Esc key
   c. click the ContextMenu button on the toolbar
   d. right-click the mouse
   e. drag and click the mouse

8. When building a context menu in Designer mode, you can change the names of the menu items by right-clicking on the menu form, and then selecting which of the following options?
   a. Edit Names
   b. Names
   c. Rename
   d. Edit Menu
   e. Edit

9. Where are the images for the buttons found on a toolbar stored?
   a. ImageControl
   b. Buttons Collection
   c. IconListControl
   d. ButtonListControl
   e. ImageListControl

10. Which property of a toolbar object determines if the toolbar can be resized to show two rows of buttons if its container is resized?
    a. Wrappable
    b. Wrap
    c. Resize
    d. CanWrap
    e. none of the above

11. Which property of a toolbar object determines if the toolbar displays a list arrow on the side of drop-down style buttons?
    a. ListArrows
    b. ShowArrows
    c. DropDownArrows
    d. Arrows
    e. ShowDropDownArrows

12. Clicking the ellipsis for the _____ property box of the ImageListControl opens the Image Collection Editor dialog box.
    a. ImageCollection
    b. Images
    c. Icons
    d. Pictures
    e. ImageList

13. Which event procedure is given control when any toolbar button is clicked for a toolbar named Toolbar1?
    a. It depends on which button was clicked on which toolbar.
    b. Toolbar1ButtonClick
    c. Toolbar1_ButtonClick
    d. Toolbar1_Click
    e. Toolbar1Button_Click

14. When an event, such as a mouse click or clicking on a button, is initiated for an object, it is said that the object _____ the event.
    a. triggers
    b. fires off
    c. instantiates
    d. raises
    e. causes

15. A text box can be set to wrap lines of text by setting which of the following text box properties to True?
    a. MultiLine
    b. Wrap
    c. Wrappable
    d. LineWrap
    e. TextWrap

16. Which file type stores data similar to the way songs are stored on an audiocassette tape?
    a. random
    b. indexed
    c. in-line
    d. sequential
    e. all of the above

17. When performing file access in a Visual Basic program, which of the following statements needs to be added to the top of the form class definition?
    a. Imports File.IO
    b. Imports IO.System
    c. File.IO = Yes
    d. File.IO = True
    e. Imports System.IO

18. To read text from a file, which type of variable needs to be declared?
    a. IOReader
    b. StreamReader
    c. TextReader
    d. TextBuffer
    e. FileReader

19. Which type of dialog box is the best to use to acquire a path name for a file to be created?
    a. OpenFileDialog
    b. FileListDialog
    c. FilePath
    d. PathList
    e. SaveFile

20. Which method of the Visual Basic StreamReader class is used to read all of the characters from a text file?
    a. ReadAll
    b. Read
    c. ReadToEnd
    d. ReadText
    e. ReadChar

MATCHING

Write the letter of the description in the right column that defines the term in the left column.

_____ 1. prompt

_____ 2. AutoSize

_____ 3. Stop

_____ 4. e

_____ 5. modal

_____ 6. Size

_____ 7. MultiLine

_____ 8. caption

_____ 9. sender

_____ 10. toolbar

a. Data type that can be declared and used to manage the height and width of a context menu

b. Type of dialog box that requires a response before the program can proceed

c. Property used with a toolbar object

d. Message box optional parameter that can be used to create a title in the message box dialog box

e. Container with rows of buttons containing icons

f. Parameter sent to an event handler that identifies the object that raised the event

g. Input box required parameter

h. A text box property that allows text to wrap

i. A parameter passed to an event handler that contains information about the event that was raised

j. An icon property that can be specified in a MessageBox statement

FILL IN THE BLANK

Complete the following sentences by writing the correct word or words in the blanks provided.

1. In the MessageBox syntax shown in the text, arguments shown in _____ are optional items.

2. The title bar of a message box dialog box displays whatever string was provided in the _____ argument for the message box.

3. In a message box statement coded to show the Yes, No, and Cancel buttons, to preselect the Yes button you code the argument: MessageBoxDefaultButton._____.

4. The InputBox function can be used to obtain information from the user; it can accept a maximum of _____ characters from the user.

5. The InputBox function displays a message prompting the user for information, a text box to enter the information, and two buttons, _____ and _____.

6. When an input box is displayed, if the user presses the Enter key without entering anything in the text box, whatever was specified as the _____ value is returned to the program.

7. If the Val() function fails in an attempt to convert a string to a value, it returns a value of _____ to the program.

8. Context menus are created for Visual Basic applications using the _____ tool.

9. _____ appear in an application as rows of buttons, each containing an icon to indicate the purpose of the button.

10. The _____ property of the toolbar object determines if ToolTips will or will not appear when the mouse pointer is positioned over a toolbar button.

11. The _____ property of the toolbar object determines the edge of the form on which the toolbar is positioned when the application is run.

12. The ToolBarButton Collection Editor dialog box can be displayed by clicking the ellipsis of the _____ property.

13. It is very important that you _____ your project whenever you step away from your computer in case the power fails or someone else accesses your machine.

14. The _____ parameter that is passed to an event handler identifies the object that initiated the event.

15. A vertical scroll bar can be added to a text box control by setting the _____ property of the text box to _____.

16. A property used to make one control match the size of another, and which is only available during runtime, is the _____ property.

17. A(n) _____ file stores data in fixed length pieces called records, where each record is the same length.

18. The _____ statement allows you to specify the name of a control in the keyword statement, and then access each property without respecifying the control name in each property statement.

19. To create a new text file from an application program, you must have a valid _____ name for the file.

20. When using the With statement in your program, each property name being referenced must be preceded by the _____ operator.

WRITTEN QUESTIONS

Write a brief answer to the following questions.

1. Provide a brief description of the MessageBox control.

2. Describe the purpose of the following MessageBox control arguments: *buttons*, *icon*, and *defaultButton*.

3. Write three MessageBox statements. All three should display some message for the user, and all three should include a caption for the dialog box. The first one should include the OK and Cancel buttons, and an Information icon. The second should include the Yes, No, and Cancel buttons, and a Warning icon. The third should include the Abort, Retry, and Ignore buttons, and an Exclamation icon. Include code statements to retrieve the return value indicating which button was clicked, and display each value in three different text boxes.

4. Write another MessageBox statement. This message box should include the Abort, Retry, and Ignore buttons. Include the Stop icon, and include the parameter to set the Retry button as the preselected button. As before, save the value returned in an integer field, and move it to a text box for display to the user.

5. Describe the purpose and the use of the InputBox function.

6. Write three InputBox statements to prompt the user for their first name, their last name, and their age. Include a title parameter, and a default value parameter for each statement. Save the returned values in three different text boxes.

7. Examine the following code statements. What would happen if the user enters alphabetic data instead of a numeric value when this code is executed? How could you change this code to account for the fact that a user may enter invalid data, and what would happen as a result of your changes if the user again entered alphabetic data instead of numeric?

```
Dim x As Integer
x = InputBox ("Please enter your zip code.")
MessageBox.Show(x.ToString)
```

8. Explain what is meant by the term *clean input*. What happens if the input is not clean? How can you fix it if it occurs?

9. What are context menus, and what would they be used for? How do you create them?

10. Describe the purpose of a toolbar and indicate the steps involved in creating a toolbar.

11. What happens when a user clicks a button on a toolbar?

PROJECT 5-1

Write a program to compute the cost of going to the movies. The GUI consists of a **Purchase** button, a **Reset** button, and an **Exit** button. When the user clicks the Purchase button, an InputBox function asks the age of the person for whom the ticket is being purchased. Make sure that the value is a valid number before you try to process it. Once you have the age of the ticket holder, add the cost of the ticket onto a variable that is keeping track of the total cost. (*Hint*: Use Form_Load to initialize the total cost variable, and define it in the Declarations section.) Use a message box to inform the user of the cost of the ticket they have just purchased and their total price so far. The pricing policy for this theater is that tickets for children under 12 cost $5.50, tickets for seniors over 55 cost $6.50, and all others cost $7.50. When the user clicks the Reset button, the variable keeping track of the total cost is reset to zero. When the user clicks the Exit button, the program ends.

Use the caption **Movie Tickets** for your form. Save the form and project as **MovieTickets** in a folder named **MovieTickets**.

PROJECT 5-2

Write a program using a toolbar to help a user choose a picture frame. Give the first button on the toolbar a caption of **Size** and a drop-down list with the following entries: **3×5**, **5×7**, **8×10**, and **11×14**. The second button's caption is **Oak**, and the third button's is **Walnut**. The fourth button exits the program. Don't worry about finding appropriate icons for the buttons, but attach icons to each button. Load the images in an ImageList control first, and then attach the ImageList to the toolbar. Make up prices for a frame of each size made with each different material.

The user selects a size first from the drop-down list, and then must click the Size button to record the selection. When the user then clicks the Oak or Walnut buttons, the program displays the price of the frame in a message box. The Toolbar1_ButtonClick event must verify that a size has been selected before a frame can be priced. You also need to set the Checked property for the drop-down menu item when selected, and clear the Checked property for the other menu items.

Give the form the caption **Choose a Picture Form**. Save the form and project in a folder named **PictureFrame**.

PROGRAMMING AT WORK

In the last lesson, you created a user interface for a medical records data entry form. In this lesson, you add features that allow the user more flexibility in how they interact with the program. Specifically, you add a pop-up menu and a toolbar that allow the user to execute the same commands that are currently executed through the buttons at the bottom of the application.

To get started, make a copy of your folder **MedicalRecords1**. Rename the copy **MedicalRecords2**. Do your work for this project in the MedicalRecords2 folder. The advantage in doing this is that you will still have a copy of your first-stage solution should anything happen to your second stage program as you are working on it. It is always good to keep backups of your programming projects, both on the computer's hard drive and on other disks.

Begin by associating some code with the Record button. The code can simply display a message box with the information that the Record button has been clicked. Create a pop-up menu with the commands **Record**, **Clear**, and **Exit** in it. Put a separator between the first two commands and the Exit option. Enter code for the menu items that makes selection of that menu item result in activation of the method associated with the corresponding button and code that makes the pop-up menu display when the user right-clicks the mouse button. Verify that your pop-up menu works correctly before going on to add the toolbar.

The toolbar provides another easy way for users to choose commands to be performed. Create a toolbar at the top of your form that allows the user to perform any of the three actions available to them. As with the pop-up menu, the code associated with a button being clicked on the toolbar is a call to the method of the corresponding button at the bottom of the form. Test that your toolbar works as expected.

LESSON 6: DATABASE PROGRAMMING

TRUE/FALSE

Circle T if the statement is true or F if the statement is false.

T F **1.** When data is organized into some useful sequence or arrangement, it becomes information.

T F **2.** The design of a database does not affect the performance of a program accessing the data in any way.

T F **3.** ODBC is a commonly used API that enables application programs to access data stored in a local database.

T F **4.** You can quickly and easily create a DSN for database access using the ODBC Data Source Administrator dialog box.

T F **5.** The acronym SQL stands for *simple query language*.

T F **6.** A Connection object's Open and Close properties grant or deny access to the specified database.

T F **7.** Applications normally do not access a database directly because many databases today are stored on a network server, and maintaining a constant connection is a waste of network resources.

T F **8.** Every column of the DataGrid control corresponds to one complete record from the database.

T F **9.** If you have edited the data in a field in the data grid, but have not pressed the Enter key or Tab key to leave the cell, you can press the Backspace key to cancel your edits.

T F **10.** You can move the focus from field to field in the data grid control by pressing the Tab key.

T F **11.** On the Connection tab of the Data Link Properties dialog box you can browse your computer or network to locate the physical database file you wish to connect to.

T F **12.** After using the Wizard to create a database connection to an OLE database, the component tray of the Designer will contain an OleDbDataAdapter object, as well as an OleDbConnection object.

T F **13.** Once a database connection is established, you must manually enter field names into the header row of the DataGrid control to identify each field.

T F **14.** You can specify a color for alternating rows of a DataGrid control by modifying its SetAlternatingColor property.

T F **15.** The TabSequence property of the DataGrid control determines the tab order of the columns within the control.

T F **16.** The Location property of the DataGrid control determines the location of the control using a variable of the Point data type.

T F **17.** Instead of displaying dataset fields in a data grid, you can create connections between the fields in the dataset and text boxes on a form to display the data one record at a time on a form.

T F **18.** When using a form to display database fields, you should have a button to load the dataset, a button to go to the next record in the dataset, and a button to go to the previous record in the dataset.

T F **19.** Visual Basic allows you to define data blocks, which are useful for representing data that is too complex to represent with a single, simple data type.

T F **20.** The definition of a UDT may include a field that is itself a UDT.

MULTIPLE CHOICE

Select the best response for the following statements.

1. A database record is subdivided into individual units of data called
   a. tables.
   b. objects.
   c. controls.
   d. fields.
   e. none of the above.

2. What does the acronym API stand for?
   a. Architectural Programming Interface
   b. Application Programming Interface
   c. Active Programming Interface
   d. Active Processor Interface
   e. Archive Processing Interface

3. In order to use ODBC with a Visual Basic application, you must create a DSN, which is an acronym for which of the following?
   a. DataSet Name
   b. Data Server Name
   c. Data Source Name
   d. Data Sequence Name
   e. Database Server Name

4. Visual Basic uses two types of connection objects to link a database with an application, the SqlConnection object and which of the following objects?
   a. ODBCConnection
   b. OleConnection
   c. AccessConnection
   d. APIConnection
   e. OleDbConnection

5. The most important property of a connection object is the _____, which provides the information necessary to access a database.
   a. ProfileObject
   b. DBObject
   c. ConnectionString
   d. SQLString
   e. DriverObject

6. Application programs do not access a DSN directly, but by means of a(n) _____, which consists of stored copies of some or all of the records in the database.
   a. dataset
   b. data pool
   c. buffer set
   d. buffer pool
   e. dataObject

7. Which of the following is a language that was developed solely for the purpose of asking questions of databases?
   a. LISP
   b. UNIX
   c. QLC
   d. SQL
   e. JAVA

8. In order to connect a DataGrid control to a dataset, which property of the DataGrid control must be set to the name of the dataset?
   a. DataSetName
   b. DataSource
   c. DataSet
   d. DataControl
   e. DataDSN

9. Which keystroke combination moves you from your current location in a data grid to the upper-left corner of the grid?
   a. Tab+Home
   b. Shift+Home
   c. Esc+Home
   d. Alt+Home
   e. Ctrl+Home

10. On which tab of the Data Link Properties dialog box would you select the type of database you are trying to connect to (which type of database engine)?
    a. Connection
    b. Provider
    c. Database
    d. Advanced
    e. DataSource

11. Which feature of the Data Adapter Configuration Wizard can you use to help create the SQL statements needed to access data in the database?
    a. SQL Starter
    b. SQL Wizard
    c. SQL Builder
    d. Query Builder
    e. Query Wizard

12. Once a database connection is established, which link appears below the Properties window and can be accessed to build a new dataset from the database file?
    a. GetDataSet
    b. BuildDataSet
    c. ViewDataSet
    d. CreateDataSet
    e. GenerateDataSet

13. Every column that is created in a DataGrid control is automatically added to which of the following collections?
   a. GridColumns
   b. DataGridColumns
   c. GridItems
   d. DataGridItems
   e. none of the above

14. Which of the following property names and associated settings allows the user to sort the data grid by clicking one of the column headers?
   a. AllowSorting - Yes
   b. AllowSorting - True
   c. SortGrid - Yes
   d. SortGrid - True
   e. SortOnColumn - True

15. When choosing a color for a font or a background, which of the following options are valid and available palettes you can choose from?
   a. Custom
   b. Web
   c. System
   d. A and B
   e. A, B, and C

16. Which property of a TextBox control can be accessed to make a connection between a specific field of a dataset and the text box?
   a. FieldBindings
   b. DataConnections
   c. DataBindings
   d. FieldConnections
   e. You cannot bind a dataset field to a text box.

17. The _____ object uses two parameters: the first is the name of the dataset it is associated with, and the second is the name of the table within the dataset that the data belongs to.
   a. CurrencyManager
   b. DataAdapter
   c. DataBindings
   d. BindingContext
   e. DataManager

18. Which property of the CurrencyManager is used to control the display of the data from the dataset?
   a. Position
   b. Count
   c. Location
   d. Record
   e. Index

19. To create a UDT, which of the following keywords would you use to identify it as a UDT?
    a. UDT
    b. Record
    c. UType
    d. NewDataType
    e. Structure

20. Assuming a UDT named Person is defined with fields named Fname, Lname, and Address, which code statement below shows the proper way for an instance of the structure named MyPerson to access the Fname field?
    a. MyPerson:Fname = "Tom"
    b. MyPerson.Fname = "Tom"
    c. MyPerson@Fname = "Tom"
    d. MyPersonFname = "Tom"
    e. MyPerson(Fname) = "Tom"

MATCHING

Write the letter of the description in the right column that defines the term in the left column.

_____ **1.** ODBC

_____ **2.** OleDbDataAdapter

_____ **3.** record

_____ **4.** ConnectionString

_____ **5.** API

_____ **6.** CurrencyManager

_____ **7.** field

_____ **8.** structure

_____ **9.** DataGrid

_____ **10.** table

a. Feature that enables programmers and users to utilize functions built into the operating system

b. One unit of information within a database record

c. Control used to display database information to the user

d. Term used to describe the structure that contains all the records for a database file

e. Control that helps you create the dataset that an application uses to access and modify data in the database

f. Property that provides the information necessary to access a database

g. User-defined data type

h. Term used to describe one row in a database file

i. Feature used to prepare a database for use in a program

j. Object that coordinates the display of multiple text boxes linked to different fields of the same dataset

FILL IN THE BLANK

Complete the following sentences by writing the correct word or words in the blanks provided.

1. Modern databases organize data fields related to each other into _____, and each database may contain more than one of these.

2. Most databases today are designed around Microsoft's _____ Server.

3. The acronym ODBC stands for Open Database _____.

4. Part of the process of creating a DSN is the selection of a(n) _____, which is a program that turns the data source into an ODBC data source.

5. A network computer that makes a database available to other computers on the network is called an SQL _____.

6. The term OLE stands for object linking and _____.

7. The OleDbDataAdapter control from the _____ panel of the Visual Basic Toolbox steps you through the process of establishing a connection between a database and the application program.

8. A DataGrid control can be set to _____ the data by specifying a particular column as the _____ field.

9. Every field in a data grid is referred to as a(n) _____.

10. Double-clicking the OleDbDataAdapter control in the Toolbox adds it to the project and causes the Data Adapter _____ _____ to appear.

11. In the Select Access Database dialog box, you can click the _____ _____ button to verify that a connection can be made to your selected database.

12. In an SQL Select statement, a(n) _____ means to select all.

13. If a database dataset has more than one table, the DataGrid control changes to show a hierarchical arrangement in which one table is the _____ to the other tables.

14. You can specify a background color for the caption bar of a DataGrid control by modifying its _____ property.

15. Setting the DataGrid control's _____ property to True means that the control cannot be resized while the application is executing.

16. When choosing a color for a font or a background, the colors that appear in the _____ palette are specially formulated to appear the same in any browser.

17. When binding text boxes to dataset fields, the _____ object coordinates the display of multiple text boxes linked to different fields of the same dataset.

18. Each field of a dataset represents one _____ of data in a data grid.

19. Visual Basic allows you to create UDTs, which stands for _____ data types.

20. Structures are often defined using the _____ keyword at the module level, which makes them accessible to all procedures and functions in the module.

WRITTEN QUESTIONS

Write a brief answer to the following questions.

1. What is a database? What are the major components of a database?

2. Name at least two factors that need to be considered when designing a database.

3. What is a DSN, and what is it used for?

4. What is a connection object, and how many types of connection objects are there in Visual Basic?

5. What is a dataset, and why would you use one instead of just accessing a database directly?

6. What is the purpose of a DataGrid control? Describe how it is used and some of its features.

7. What is the DataBindings property of a text box used for?

8. What is a UDT, and why would a programmer want to create one?

9. Write the code statements required to create a UDT named *Employee*. This UDT should contain the employee's id number, their first and last names, their department code, and the year they were hired.

10. Write the code statements necessary to initialize one instance of the *Employee* object you created in Question 9. Use your name as the employee name and make up the data for the other fields.

PROJECT 6-1

Create a database using Access or some other database accessible by Visual Basic. Create a table to record information about your favorite automobiles. Include **Model**, **Make**, **Style** (4-door, coupe, SUV, etc.), **List Price**, **Features**, and **Comments**, with all fields required except Features and Comments. Enter data for at least five autos. You can find real data for this problem in auto magazines or a local newspaper. Name the database **AutoInfo** and store it in a folder named **AutoInfo**.

Once your database is created, write a program to connect the AutoInfo database to a Visual Basic project. Create a form with text boxes and labels to display each field in the database in text boxes, allowing the user to edit data and navigate back and forth to each record.

Name the project **AutoInfo** and save it in the **AutoInfo** folder.

PROJECT 6-2

Using Access or some comparable database system, build a database of hobbies and interests for family members. Create a single database table. Each record in the table stores the person's first name and up to five hobbies or interests. The name and first hobby field are required. Other hobby fields are optional. Use the Data Form Wizard to build a form to access the database. When prompted for a form layout, use the Grid (Datasheet) layout with all the fields added. Store all your work in a folder named **Hobbies**.

PROJECT 6-3

Write a program with a UDT to save information about baseball cards. The program lets the user read and write a text file of baseball cards, and display all the cards using Next and Previous buttons.

The baseball card UDT contains a player's name, current team, and current number. Create an array of the structure object and pick a constant (such as 20) to use as the maximum number of cards that can be in the array of objects. When adding data, verify that there is space in the array that is storing the database before adding a new item.

Add labels to the form to identify each field, and add text boxes to the form in which to display the field data. Add a menu to the form with **File** and **Data** titles. The File menu should have **New**, **Open File**, **Save As**, and **Exit** options. The Data menu should have **Clear Card**, **Add Card**, and **Display Cards** options. When the user clicks the New option, clear the current array and the text boxes to allow the user to create a new set of cards. The Open File and Save As options require an OpenFileDialog control and a SaveFileDialog control. Consult the Lesson 6 text to create these event procedures. The user can save the current array to a file at any time, and can open an existing file to load the array.

The Clear Card option on the Data menu simply clears the data from the form's text boxes. The Add Card option allows the user to enter new data in the text boxes, and when a user clicks the Add Card menu item, it adds the new data to the end of the existing array. Make sure there is room to add it. You need to keep two counters. One contains the total number of cards currently in the array, and the other is an index to the currently displayed card, if browsing the array. The Display Cards option sets the current card counter to the beginning of the array (do not reset the last card counter) and displays the data in the array, if any, in the text boxes on the form.

Add a **Next** and a **Previous** button to the form. These should be disabled when adding cards to the form, or when the Clear Card or New option is invoked. When the Display Cards option is clicked, then these two buttons need to be enabled to let the user browse each entry. The event procedures for these buttons need to check that there is data in the array, and that they are not at the end for the Next button, or at the beginning for the Previous button. Save the project as **BaseballCards** in a folder of the same name.

PROGRAMMING AT WORK

In the previous two Programming at Work sections, you created a user interface for a medical record data storage program. In this stage of the program, you create a small database of patient information, and then you connect that database to the form you have created. As in the last activity, you should make a copy of your folder named **MedicalRecords2** and rename that **MedicalRecords3**. Your work for this phase of the program should be done using the files in MedicalRecords3.

The first thing that must be done if you are going to connect this form to a database is that a database to connect it to must be created. Use Access or some comparable database system to create a database named **Patients**. Create a new table in the database named **PatientInfo** that has a field corresponding to each of the entries on your Patient Information Entry form. The required information is the Id number, both name components, and the insurance provider. The fields should all be text fields. Once you have established the fields, build the table, and then add at least four made-up entries into your database. After you have added the four patients, you can close the database and move on to connecting the database to your form.

Use the OleDbDataAdapter control to establish a relationship with the database. Create a dataset named **DsPatientInfo**. Use the DataBindings property to associate each field in the database with its corresponding field on the form. You need to add three command buttons to the form. Add a button with the text **Load**, one with the text **Next**, and one with the text **Previous**. Add appropriate code for each button using the same techniques you learned in the Lesson 6 text.

After all code is entered, build and run the project. Click the **Load** button. All text boxes should be filled in with the information contained in the first record of the database you created. Click the **Next** button to cycle through all the records, and then click the **Previous** button until you return to the first record in the database.

Save all of your changes and close the project.

LESSON 7:   DEBUGGING AND SIMPLE CLASSES

TRUE/FALSE

Circle T if the statement is true or F if the statement is false.

T   F   **1.** If you plan your application very carefully, you never have to worry about a user crashing your program.

T   F   **2.** When asking a user to enter a date or a dollar amount, the prompt to the user should indicate the pattern or format to use to input the value.

T   F   **3.** Depending on which compiler option is set, if you enter the name of an undeclared variable in a code statement, Visual Basic marks the variable name with a jagged underline.

T   F   **4.** Visual Basic's Option Protect compiler option allows for widening conversions when it is turned on.

T   F   **5.** When executing your program in Visual Basic step mode, you can single-step through each code statement and examine the results of each operation.

T   F   **6.** If you select the Start Without Debugging option on the Debug menu, you cannot set breakpoints in the code.

T   F   **7.** When a program reaches a breakpoint, if you hover the mouse pointer over a variable name, a ToolTip appears displaying the current value of the variable.

T   F   **8.** If you start your program by clicking the Start Without Debugging option on the Debug menu and the program encounters a run-time error, you are given the option of trying to continue, or of entering break mode to fix the problem.

T   F   **9.** When you enter break mode, the Debugger window replaces the output window that is visible during the application's building process.

T   F   **10.** With a large program, it is often easier to debug the program using one or more watch expressions instead of using breakpoints or single-stepping the code.

T   F   **11.** The Step Over command allows you to execute a block or function of code without single-stepping when you know that the code in that function is error-free and not part of the problem you are tracing.

T   F   **12.** When creating data to test an application, you need to include data that tests boundary conditions, the largest and smallest values, negative values, and any other extreme conditions that you can think of.

T   F   **13.** When using the Try-Catch-Finally statement to process errors, there can only be one Try clause, one Catch clause, and one Finally clause.

T   F   **14.** An instance of a class refers to all of the code statements and variables defined for that class.

T   F   **15.** Adding a method to a newly created class is just as easy as adding an event procedure for a control.

MULTIPLE CHOICE

Select the best response for the following statements.

1. Which of the following terms refers to the process of catching a run-time error and routing it to special code designed to handle that type of error?
   a. rerouting
   b. error routing
   c. error trapping
   d. code diversion
   e. exception routing

2. Which of the following statements causes Visual Basic to flag an undeclared variable as soon as you press the Enter key at the end of the line where the variable is referenced?
   a. Variable Checking
   b. Option Check
   c. Explicit Checking
   d. Option Explicit On
   e. Flag Unknown

3. Which of the following terms describes the process of converting a variable of Integer data type to a variable of Decimal data type?
   a. widening conversion
   b. promotion
   c. data swapping
   d. type swapping
   e. data translation

4. The Visual Basic IDE allows you to specify _____, which are spots in the code where execution pauses to allow you to examine and/or modify variables.
   a. code traps
   b. code breaks
   c. step points
   d. breakpoints
   e. code windows

5. To single-step through a Visual Basic program, you first select Debug on the menu bar, and then you select which of the following options?
   a. Code Step
   b. Single Step
   c. Step By Step
   d. Single Cycle
   e. Step Into

6. When a breakpoint has been set in a Visual Basic program, what symbol appears in the channel on the edge of the Code window?
   a. an exclamation point
   b. a round ball
   c. an asterisk
   d. an at sign
   e. none of the above

7. How do you remove a breakpoint when you no longer need it?
   a. Click the breakpoint symbol in the channel of the Code window.
   b. Click the Debug menu, and then click Remove Breakpoint.
   c. Click the Debug menu, and then click Clear All Breakpoints.
   d. both a and c
   e. none of the above

8. What is the correct name for the arrow that indicates where an error occurs when you enter break mode due to a run-time error?
   a. Error Pointer
   b. Error Indicator
   c. Current Instruction Pointer
   d. Current Position Indicator
   e. Error Location Indicator

9. In which of the following Visual Basic debugging modes can you enter expressions to evaluate variables, display the current value of variables, and set the values of variables?
   a. Immediate mode
   b. Command mode
   c. Control mode
   d. Interactive mode
   e. any of the above

10. When a watch expression has been set, which window displays the watch expression when the program enters break mode?
    a. Immediate window
    b. Command window
    c. Breakpoint window
    d. Watch window
    e. Output window

11. Which statement can be included in a Visual Basic application to cause it to ignore run-time errors?
    a. On Error Skip
    b. On Error Resume Next
    c. On Error Step Over
    d. On Error Ignore
    e. On Error Jump Over

12. In a Try-Catch-Finally statement, the _____ portion of the Catch statement is used to distinguish between conditions and to provide appropriate statements that respond to the error based on the condition.
    a. How
    b. Where
    c. Why
    d. What
    e. When

13. Where can you see a complete list of all methods and properties of a class?
    a. Class Window
    b. Methods Window
    c. Object Browser
    d. Class Browser
    e. Solution Explorer

14. Which of the following Visual Basic menus has an option that allows you to add a new class to a project?
    a. Project
    b. Build
    c. Tools
    d. Edit
    e. none of the above

15. Which of the following options correctly identifies the two parts of the Err object that is maintained by the system to contain information about a recent error?
    a. .Description and .Time
    b. .Description and .Number
    c. .LineNumber and .Variable
    d. .ErrCode and .LineNumber
    e. .Description and .LineNumber

MATCHING

Write the letter of the description in the right column that defines the term in the left column.

_____ 1. Current Instruction Pointer	a. An unintentional or unknown error within a program
_____ 2. Immediate	b. One or more variables that can be set that causes the program to enter break mode when it changes
_____ 3. When	c. Simple debugging tool that minimizes the possibility of creating multiple variable names to refer to the same object
_____ 4. breakpoint	
_____ 5. Command	d. Something that causes a program to enter break mode only when a specific value or condition is reached or exceeded
_____ 6. watch expression	
_____ 7. bug	e. An arrow indicating the current line of code being executed when the program enters break mode
_____ 8. Finally	f. Part of a Catch statement used to identify different conditions to be trapped
_____ 9. conditional breakpoint	
_____ 10. InterCap naming convention	g. Code executed if no error is found in a Try clause, or executed after the error has been processed
	h. Mode in which you can enter expressions and display or modify variables
	i. Line or area of code where the program enters break mode each time it is executed
	j. Window that appears in place of the Output window when you enter break mode

FILL IN THE BLANK

Complete the following sentences by writing the correct word or words in the blanks provided.

1. An unintended programming error in an application program is referred to as a(n) _____.

2. A control named btnOpenFile has been named using the _____ naming convention, which is an easy-to-use debugging tool.

3. Visual Basic's Option _____ compiler option prevents the value of one variable from being assigned to some other variable if the assignment would cause a loss of data.

4. Misspelling a command name, or a variable name, or omitting a required parameter or statement, are all examples of _____ errors.

5. A Visual Basic program automatically enters _____ mode if it encounters a run-time error.

6. Visual Basic breakpoints are set in the _____ channel on the _____ edge of the Code window.

7. In addition to setting breakpoints in the channel of the Code window, you can also set them by clicking in the line where the breakpoint should occur, and then selecting the _____ option from the Debug menu.

8. If a run-time error occurs and you enter break mode, a(n) _____ arrow in the left margin indicates the line where the error occurred.

9. If you are in the Command window, you can switch to the Immediate window by entering _____ at the > prompt of the Command window.

10. When a program is paused in break mode, you can resume execution of the program by selecting the _____ option on the Debug menu.

11. A(n) _____ breakpoint allows you to define an expression that causes the program to enter break mode when the condition reaches or exceeds some particular value.

12. When using the Try-Catch-Finally statement, the code in the _____ section is executed. If no error occurs, control is given to the _____ section, or else it is given to the _____ section.

13. In addition to using breakpoints and single-stepping through code, another commonly used debugging technique is to create an error _____, which is a file where the program lists errors that occurred and the time that they occurred.

14. A class is a definition from which a(n) _____ is created.

15. When you add a new class to a project, Visual Basic supplies a basic framework, and then you add _____ such as methods and variables to complete the class.

WRITTEN QUESTIONS

Write a brief answer to the following questions.

1. Describe the Visual Basic terms *Option Explicit On* and *Option Strict.* In addition to describing what they are, explain how they are used or activated.

2. What is the purpose or benefit of using breakpoints?

3. How do you set a breakpoint, and how do you know where the breakpoints are once they have been set?

4. How can you remove a breakpoint once it has been set?

5. Explain the difference between running a program using the Debug | Start, and the Debug | Start Without Debugging options?

6. When you are in break mode, how can you determine what value is currently contained in a variable?

7. What is the difference between a breakpoint and a conditional breakpoint?

8. What is the purpose of the Try-Catch-Finally statement? How does it work?

9. Explain the difference between the Step Into and the Step Over debugging commands?

10. What is the purpose of an error log?

11. What is the difference between a class and an object?

PROJECT 7-1

Write a program that lets the user enter a series of numbers, and displays the sum of the numbers and the average of the numbers when the user clicks on a button. Name the project **Average**, in a folder with the same name.

Specifically, create a user interface with three labels and four text boxes. The first text box contains a number to be added to the total of the numbers entered so far. The second text box reports the sum of the numbers, and the third reports the average of the numbers. Each text box has a corresponding label describing its contents. The application has four buttons, **Add Number**, **Compute**, **Reset**, and **Exit**. In addition, two integer variables must be declared in the General Declarations section of the code for this program. Appropriate names for the variables are **intTotal** and **intCount**.

When Add Number is clicked, the number currently displayed in the number text box is added to intTotal, and intCount is incremented by one. Also, the following two lines of code should be added after the update of the two variables, assuming you have named your text box for the next number *txtNumber*:

```
txtNumber.Text = ""
txtNumber.Focus()
```

As you know, the first line makes the number text box blank. The second puts the input cursor into the text box, so that the next typing automatically goes into that box. That is, the user does not have to click on the text box to be able to put input into it after adding a number.

When Compute is clicked, the value of intTotal is written into the sum text box first, and then the average of the numbers (intTotal/intCount) is written into the average text box. The Reset button sets all three text box fields to blank and also sets intTotal and intCount both back to zero. The Exit button terminates the program.

Once you have written the program, test it with a few different series of numbers to be sure it is computing the average correctly. When you are sure it is computing the average correctly, enter the Code window if it is not already visible. Add breakpoints to the first code statement in the Click procedures for the Add Number button, the Compute button, and the Reset button. Start the program using debugging, enter a number into the text box, and click the Add Number button. When you enter break mode, examine all the variables and their values by hovering the mouse pointer over the variable names in the code. You can also use the Autos window to examine the current values. If it is not visible in the lower-left corner, click the **Debug** menu, click **Other Windows**, and then click **Autos**.

Press the **F11** key to single-step through the remainder of the function and watch as the values change when each line is executed. Add several more numbers into the form and watch as each one is processed in the Click procedure for the Add Number button. Click the Compute button after you have entered three or four numbers and single-step through that Click procedure. Do the same thing for the Reset button. When you have single-stepped through each Click procedure, click the Exit button to end the program. Save all of your changes and exit the project.

PROJECT 7-2

Create a new project named **LoopTest**, in a folder of the same name. Add a button to the form. Name the button **btnStart**, and change the Text property to **Start Loop**. Add a second button below the Start Loop button, name it **btnExit**, and change the Text property to **Exit**. Add a list box control to the right of the button and drag its lower border to very near the bottom of the form so that it fills almost the entire height of the form. Name the list box **lstBox1**.

Double-click the **Exit** button and add the command **End** to its Click procedure. Select **btnStart** from the Class Name list box, and **Click** from the Method Name list box. Enter the following code to declare a variable and execute a loop.

```
Dim intCnt As Integer
intCnt = 1
lstBox1.Items.Clear()
Do While intCnt <> 100
    lstBox1.Items.Add(intCnt.ToString)
    lstBox1.Show()
    intCnt += 2
Loop
```

Note that the loop only terminates if the value of intCnt is equal to 100. Also note that intCnt is initialized to a value of 1, and is incremented by 2 each time through the loop. The intCnt variable is never equal to 100, thus creating an infinite loop. When creating loops in Visual Basic programs, you can use the conditional breakpoint when testing the loop to be sure you do not create an infinite loop.

Position the mouse pointer anywhere in the line *intCnt += 2* and click the mouse to set the pointer there. Click the **Debug** menu, and then select **New Breakpoint**. Click the **File** tab, and then click the **Condition** button. In the text box in the Breakpoint Condition dialog box, enter **intCnt > 100**. This causes a breakpoint to occur on that line if intCnt exceeds a value of 100. Click **OK** twice to close the breakpoint dialog boxes.

Click the **Debug** menu, and click the **Start** option. When the form displays, click the **Start Loop** button. The program should very quickly go into break mode on the line where you set the conditional breakpoint. Position the mouse pointer over the word *intCnt* and a ToolTip appears showing you that the value of the variable is currently 101. You know that if you just continue execution this loop never ends. If the Command window is not visible in the lower-right portion of the screen, click the **View** menu, select **Other Windows**, and then select **Command Window**. When the Command window opens, position the cursor next to the > prompt, and enter **immed** to switch to the Immediate window. Enter **intCnt = 98** in the Immediate window, and then enter **>cmd** to switch back to the Command window. Position the pointer over the intCnt variable again, and now the ToolTip should show a value of 98 instead of 101. Press the **F11** key four times to finish the loop processing. Clear the breakpoint, and save and exit the program. You have just used a conditional breakpoint to detect an error in a loop.

PROGRAMMING AT WORK

In this phase of the project, you make another copy of the medical records project used in previous lessons and convert the database file to a text file. In the next lesson, you incorporate data entry and update into the project, but for now you modify the program to read in the database records, write them to an internal UDT array, and then write the array data to a text file. Copy the **MedicalRecords3** folder from Lesson 6 to a new folder **MedicalRecords4**, and open the project.

At the bottom of the form, change the Text property of the Record button to read **Copy to Array**, and change its name to **btnCopy**. Double-click it to open the Code window, find all references to btnRecord, and change them to **btnCopy**. Return to the form and change the Text property for the Previous button to **Create File**, and change its name to **btnCreate**. Open the Code window and delete all references to btnPrevious including the event handler for that button. You create a new Click event procedure for the Create button later. Arrange the buttons so from the left edge of the form you have them in this order: Load, Next, Copy to Array, Create File, Clear, and Exit.

Click on the form to select it, and drag the sizing handle on the right side of the form to the right to enlarge the form about an inch or two. Add two labels and two buttons to the right side of the current text boxes. The text for the first label should read **Records in Database**, and one of the new text boxes should be positioned immediately below the label. Name the text box **txtDbCnt**, and clear its Text property. Position the second label somewhere below the text box and change the label's text property to **Records Copied to Array**. Position the second text box below it, name the text box **txtCopyCnt**, and then clear its Text property.

At the top of the form module, create a user-defined data type for the fields contained in the current patient database. Then create an array of 20 elements of that data type. The code to construct and manage the array is very similar to the code you used in the **BaseballCards** project in the Lesson 6 activities.

Modify the current program so that when it starts, the user must click the Load button to load the database dataset first. If they try to click any other button before they click Load (with the exception of Clear or Exit), issue a message that they must first load the dataset. When the user does click the Load button, the current code in the Load procedure executes to fill the dataset. Add code to get the Count property value and copy it to the txtDbCnt text box to indicate how many records are in the database overall. Set the txtCopyCnt text box to a value of zero, and indicate (using a global Boolean value) the database is now loaded. This Boolean value can then be checked in the Next, Copy, and Create File Click procedures to see if the dataset has been loaded or not.

Once it has been loaded, the user can then click the Copy button to copy the current record to the internal array. The Copy Click procedure also must increment the count displayed in the txtCopyCnt text box. Before copying the record, this procedure should check to see if all of the database records have already been copied. If the txtDbCnt value and the txtCopyCnt values are equal, all records have been copied and you should display a message indicating all records are already in the array.

You need to add a SaveFileDialog control to the form, and set it up as you did in the BaseballCards project (see Lesson 6 activities). In this program it is set up in the Create Click procedure. When the user clicks the Create File button, make sure there are records in the array. Open a dialog box asking the user to name the file and destination folder, and then copy all array data to the text file. The first record added to the file should be a count of how many records are contained in the array. Save all changes and run the project.

Note: You do not need to modify the toolbar buttons or code for this project. They are not used in this project, but do not delete the toolbar or the buttons. They are used again in a later version of this project.

LESSON 8: CLASSES AND OBJECTS

TRUE/FALSE

Circle T if the statement is true or F if the statement is false.

T F 1. Visual Basic .NET was designed so some programs written in it are able to run on hardware and operating systems other than those in which they were created.

T F 2. An object is nothing more than a container for data.

T F 3. In an OOP environment, the operations that can be performed on objects are called methods.

T F 4. In OOP, a programmer needs to know all of the details about an object to create efficient and useful application programs.

T F 5. The class definition determines the methods, events, and properties that are associated with an object.

T F 6. The right pane of the Object Browser window shows the methods and properties of whatever class or structure has been selected in the left pane.

T F 7. Variables declared in a class as Public are not available to any procedure or program outside the class.

T F 8. When you need to redimension an array to add an additional item, it is best to just increase the size of the array by one each time you need a new slot.

T F 9. An array with no capacity is called an empty object.

T F 10. A variable defined in a class as Private is not available to anyone outside the class.

T F 11. Defining Private variables in a class module is equivalent to adding properties to the objects created with the class.

T F 12. When defining a new class, you can write the rules that govern the object into the class definition itself.

T F 13. When adding an event to a class, Visual Basic automatically adds the code to the class definition to raise the event.

T F 14. In Visual Basic, it is possible to repackage an existing object into a new class definition to improve the processing of the object for a specific situation.

T F 15. In Visual Basic, there is no difference between a function and a procedure.

MULTIPLE CHOICE

Select the best response for the following statements.

1. Code that can be used in more than one program is called what?
   a. recyclable
   b. reentrant
   c. redundant
   d. reusable
   e. repeatable

2. Which of the following OOP terms refers to the ability to hide information about an object from the user and also the programmer?
   a. Data Invisibility
   b. Data Encapsulation
   c. Data Inheritance
   d. Polymorphism
   e. Data Cloaking

3. Which term refers to redefining methods, properties, and operations to behave differently with different objects?
   a. Data Encapsulation
   b. Inheritance
   c. Data Hiding
   d. Object Evolution
   e. Polymorphism

4. The _____ allows you to examine classes and the properties of the objects created from those classes.
   a. Solution Explorer
   b. Class Explorer
   c. Object Browser
   d. Class Browser
   e. Object Explorer

5. A class definition can contain which of the following types of procedures that can be used to let the program control values that are stored in the object and retrieved from the object?
   a. Protection
   b. Property
   c. Process
   d. both a and b
   e. none of the above

6. What is the purpose of the Visual Basic ReDim command?
   a. It is used to define a reentrant variable.
   b. It creates a new copy of a variable defined in some other procedure.
   c. It redefines an existing variable of one data type to a new data type.
   d. It changes the size of an array.
   e. none of the above

7. Which of the following is a built-in constant in Visual Basic that represents an empty object?
   a. Nothing
   b. Empty
   c. Nil
   d. Vacant
   e. None

8. Which of the following functions can be used to determine the current capacity of an array object?
   a. Size()
   b. Capacity()
   c. Ubound()
   d. Len()
   e. MaxLen()

9. Which statement shows the correct way to create an object named MyCar, which is an instance of a class named Car?
   a. Instance MyCar of Class Car
   b. Dim MyCar As Car
   c. Obj MyCar As New Car
   d. Dim MyCar As Class(Car)
   e. Dim MyCar As New Car

10. A(n) _____ is an action that an object can perform.
    a. macro
    b. method
    c. instance
    d. event procedure
    e. none of the above

11. To use a MessageBox statement in a class definition, you must first import which of the following?
    a. System.IO
    b. System.WinForms
    c. System.Dialog
    d. System.Forms
    e. System.Objects

12. When declaring object variables for an event within a class definition, you must use which of the following keywords?
    a. ForEvents
    b. AsEvent
    c. ThisEvent
    d. WhenEvents
    e. WithEvents

13. Which keyword can be used in a parameter list to pass the actual address of a variable or object to a called function or method, enabling the called routine to change the actual variable or object?
    a. ByVal
    b. ByAdr
    c. ByObj
    d. ByRef
    e. ByData

14. A function is required to have which of the following statements that a procedure does not need to have?
    a. Return
    b. GoTo
    c. Send
    d. Route
    e. Jump

15. Which section of a Property procedure is called when the property is read?
    a. Return
    b. Read
    c. Get
    d. Access
    e. Retrieve

MATCHING

Write the letter of the description in the right column that defines the term in the left column.

_____ **1.** inheritance

_____ **2.** Get

_____ **3.** encapsulation

_____ **4.** polymorphism

_____ **5.** StrConv

_____ **6.** Trim$

_____ **7.** reusable

_____ **8.** Set

_____ **9.** function

_____ **10.** object

a. Section of a Property procedure called when a property needs to be written

b. Code that can be incorporated into more than one program

c. Something that contains both data and operations to be performed on the data

d. Section of a Property procedure called when a property needs to be read

e. Function used to remove leading or trailing spaces from a string

f. Method that returns a value to the caller

g. Function used to format a string

h. Creating a new class from an existing class

i. Redefining methods so that they behave differently with different objects

j. Hiding data from the user or programmer

FILL IN THE BLANK

Complete the following sentences by writing the correct word or words in the blanks provided.

1. When a program is designed to work on different _____, it means it can run on a variety of hardware and operating systems.

2. OOP is an acronym that stands for _____ programming.

3. _____ is the principle of creating a new class from an existing class, and the new class automatically has all of the properties of the original class.

4. Operator _____ refers to the ability of the existing operators for an object to have more than one function, depending on the context.

5. A container that holds the class definitions needed to create objects, such as System.IO used to create objects to access files, is called a(n) _____.

6. When you select a class or structure in the left pane of the Object Browser window, a(n) _____ of the object appears at the bottom of the window.

7. If an object named Car has a property named Model that was defined using a Property procedure, you would access the value of the property using the expression _____.

8. When you execute a command to redimension an array, you can retain the data currently in the array by using the _____ keyword.

9. When used with the StrCnv() function, the built-in constant _____ formats the passed string with an uppercase character as the first character in every word in the string, and the remaining letters in each word are in lowercase format.

10. When debugging a new class definition, you can set a breakpoint at the beginning of the code, and single-step through each statement by pressing the _____ key.

11. Adding _____ procedures to a class module is equivalent to adding methods to the objects created with the class.

12. An event procedure declared and defined within a class definition is called an event _____.

13. Using the keyword _____ in a parameter list causes the value of the parameter to be sent to the called function or method, but the called routine cannot change the actual variable or object referenced in the parameter list.

14. The _____ keyword is used to fire off control to an event handler procedure created in a class definition.

15. A rule of the workplace that is written into the code of a program is referred to as a(n) _____ _____.

WRITTEN QUESTIONS

Write a brief answer to the following questions.

1. Describe the OOP concepts of data encapsulation, inheritance, and polymorphism.

2. Is a class the same thing as a structure? If not, what is different about them?

3. What is a Property procedure? Describe its structure in Visual Basic .NET?

4. How can an array be resized once it has been created? How can you tell how large an array currently is before attempting to resize it?

5. Give a brief description of the steps involved in adding an event to a class definition.

6. What is the difference in declaring an event procedure parameter with the _ByVal_ keyword versus the _ByRef_ keyword?

PROJECT 8-1

In this and the next project, you develop a program for simple interactive banking. You also use this program in later lessons. The final program reads a file of customers and allows the user to add customers, delete customers, and open the file of current customers to perform withdrawals and deposits. The data maintained for each customer is their first and last names, an account number, and their current balance. In this phase of the program, you construct the user interface, begin creating the class to represent a customer, and implement the file operations. Use **Bank** as the name for the form, and store the files in a folder named **BankClass1**.

The user interface consists of three menus and six labels. Three of the labels contain the words **Customer Name:**, **Account Number:**, and **Balance:**. The other three labels are initially blank and later display data about a selected customer. The layout of the labels is in two columns, one column for the filled labels and the other for the blank labels.

The three menus are **File**, **Customer**, and **Transaction**. They contain the following options:

File	Customer	Transaction
New	Create New	Deposit
Open	Open Old	Withdrawal
Save	Edit Name	
[separator bar]	Delete Current	
Exit	[separator bar]	
	Previous	
	Next	

Each menu option has an appropriate access key. Create this interface, and implement the Exit option so it terminates the program.

Next, create a class module named **clsCustomer** to represent a bank customer. The properties associated with a customer are the customer's first and last names (**FName**, **LName**), account number (**AcctNumber**), and account balance (**Balance**). Use public property procedures to implement the four properties. Because you are using property procedures, use private variables in the class module to store the values of the properties. Use the Set property procedure to assign a value to the corresponding private variable, and return the value of the private variable corresponding to the property in the Get procedure.

Once the properties of the class are operational, implement the Create New option in the Customer menu. Begin by declaring an array Customers of intMaxCusts customers, where intMaxCusts is a constant with a value of 5. Also declare a variable intTotalCusts to keep track of the next empty location in the array. This variable must be initialized to 0 in the form's Load procedure. In addition, declare a variable intCurrCust and initialize it to -1 in the Load procedure. When Create New is selected, add a new customer to the array, if there is room. Be sure to transform the first and last name into standard name form (no spaces, first letter only capitalized). Set intCurrCust to the index of the customer just inserted.

Once the customer is created, display the information in the labels in the second column of the form. Write the name in the order of first and then last. Because this action will be done frequently, write a public procedure DisplayCustomer that receives an integer as input and displays the information for that customer in the form. Also write a public procedure named ClearDisplay to empty each display label, and call this when the display needs to be cleared. Call the procedure DisplayCustomer at the end of the code for Create New, sending intCurrCust as the input value.

Implement the Previous and Next options by exiting if there is not a current customer; that is, intCurrCust is equal to -1. Otherwise change the value to one less or one greater, and display the new customer. These operations wrap around the array. That is, if intCurrCust is zero when Previous is clicked, display the last customer in the array, in position intTotalCustomers -1, and similarly for Next.

To complete this phase of the project, add code to implement the File menu items using the OpenFileDialog and SaveFileDialog controls. Use the file extension .bnk for the filter for the data files. The New option sets intTotalCusts back to 0, intCurrCust to -1, and clears the customer display labels. The Open option reads the data about each customer into the customer array and, if the file was not empty, sets intCurrCust to 0 and displays that customer. If the file was empty, the customer display labels are cleared. The Save procedure writes the information about each customer in the array to the selected file in the order Last Name, First Name, Account Number, and Balance. The first record written to the file when saving the array should be a count of the objects in the array, and the first record read when opening the file is the count of objects in the file.

Test that your implementation works so far by inputting several customers, saving to a file, and looking at the file. Make a new file, add some customers, and save that file. Close your program and restart it. Read in one of your previously created files, and save it to a file with a new name. Check that the data in the new file is the same as the data in the one you opened. Put in more than five customers to test that the code for too many customers works correctly. Use the Previous and Next options. Verify that the wrap around for these is working.

PROJECT 8-2

In this project, you complete the banking exercise you began in Project 8-1. Begin by copying the folder **BankClassl** to a new folder named **BankClass2**. Do your work for this program in the BankClass2 folder.

Open the Code window for frmBank, and change intMaxCusts from 5 to 20. To implement the Open Old item in the Customer menu, you must first write a procedure that takes a first and last name as inputs and searches for an account that has that name associated with it. The heading for this procedure is:

```
Public Sub LocateName(ByVal strFirst As String, ByVal strLast As String)
```

The procedure does a sequential search through the customer array. If an account with the given name is found, the global variable intCurrCust is set to the index of the account in the array. If no such name is found, the variable is set to -1.

The Open Old item uses this procedure by first getting the first and last names from the user (in standard form) and then calling LocateName. If after LocateName the value of intCurrCust is -1, Open Old displays a message that an account with that name was not found. Otherwise, Open Old writes the information from the location in the customer array indicated by intCurrCust to the corresponding label fields in the form.

Implement Edit Name by getting a new first and last name from the user, and resetting the name properties of the current customer if the input is not the null string. Display the new name and the other account information in the form. After completing the edit, use a message box to explain that to make the modification permanent, the account file must be saved. Ask if the user wants to save the file now. If yes, call the procedure that saves a file. Error checking that must be done before performing any operations are to verify that there are customers currently in the array and that intCurrCust is not –1; that is, there is a customer displayed. If either of these occurs, display an appropriate message and exit the subroutine.

Implement Delete Current. First check if the customer in position intCurrCust is the last one in the array. If it is, deletion occurs by deleting one from intTotalCusts. If it is not, then put the customer in the last position in the array into position intCurrCust. Then subtract one from intTotalCusts. If there are any customers left in the array, set the current customer to the one in position 0 and display the customer. Verify making the changes permanent, and perform error checking similar to that in the Edit Name code.

Finally, implement the Transaction menu options Deposit and Withdrawal. These only activate if there are customers in the array and if the current customer is set. Each calls the corresponding method for the current customer and then displays the current customer. However, the methods that must be called have not been written yet! Open the Code window for your customer class file, and add a public procedure named MakeDeposit. This method prompts the user for an amount of a deposit. If the deposit amount is larger than or equal to 0, add the amount to the balance. If it is less than 0, display a message stating that negative deposits are not allowed, and to use withdrawal instead. Add a similar method named MakeWithdrawal. Once you have written these, return to the Code window for frmBank, and implement the Deposit and Withdrawal items.

Test your program extensively to be sure that all the features you added work correctly.

PROGRAMMING AT WORK

In this project you replace the remaining sections of the medical records program that still use the original database. The program is changed to read the text patient data file that was created and saved in the previous lesson's activities. Copy the contents of the **MedicalRecords4** folder to a folder named **MedicalRecords5**. You use that folder to make the changes described here.

Open the project and delete the **OleDbDataAdapter** control, the **OleDbConnection** control, and the **DsPatientInfo** controls from the project. Add an **OpenFileDialog** control to the project. Change the text of the Load button to **Load File**, and double-click the button to enter that event procedure. Remove any code associated with the data set for the database file. Do not remove the DbLoaded reference. Although we will now be using a text file, the data is still a database as it contains organized information. Modify the Load procedure to use the OpenFileDialog control and ask the user to locate and open the text file. When the file is opened, load the array with the data in the file. Remember, the first record in the file contains the count of the number of records in the file.

After the array is loaded, set the current patient variable to a value of last patient - 1. This fools the Next routine into thinking it is at the end of the array, and forces it to wrap around to the beginning of the array. The btnLoad_Click event procedure should call the btnNext_Click procedure to copy the first record in the array into the text boxes on the form.

Locate the btnNext_Click procedure in the Code window. Remove any code pertaining to the database file, including the references to the Position property. Modify the procedure to first check the DbLoaded variable to make certain the array has been loaded before trying to display the next record. Then, check the current patient variable. If it is not at the last patient in the array, increment it by one and load the text boxes with the data from the array using the current patient index value. If the current patient is equal to the last entry in the array, set it to zero, and display the first patient in the array.

Return to the form itself, and change the name of the _Copy the Array_ button to **btnPrevious**. Change the Text property to **&Previous**. Locate the old **Copy** event procedure and delete it from the Code window. Select the **btnPrevious** object from the Class Name box, and **Click** from the Method Name box. Create a Previous routine similar to the next procedure, but if the current patient is zero (beginning of the array), set the current patient index equal to the index for the last entry in the array. If the current patient is not zero, decrease the current patient value by one and load the text boxes.

On the right side of the form, modify the Text property of the Records in Database label to **Total Record Count**. Leave the name of the txtDbCnt text box as is. Change the Text property of the **Records Copied to Array** label to **Current Record**. Change the name of the text box below it from *txtCopyCnt* to **txtCurrent**. Add a statement to the btnLoad_Click event procedure to set the txtDbCnt.Text property to the value of LastPatient. Change the event procedures for the Next and Previous buttons to set the txtCurrent.Text property to the value of CurPatient plus one. You are using "CurPatient plus one" to show the record number relative to one, which most users would understand easier than referencing array variables relative to zero as a programmer is used to doing. Remember, you are creating this program for a user, not for yourself.

Feel free to rearrange the buttons and/or text boxes if you want to change the form design slightly. Test all of your changes and save all project files. When you are satisfied that the program is working as it should, close the project and exit Visual Basic. Although we have not addressed the current toolbar buttons and are not using the toolbar button code at this time, do not delete it. You will be adding additional functionality to this program in a later lesson and the toolbar is addressed at that time.

LESSON 9:   EXPLORING ALL KINDS OF COLLECTIONS

TRUE/FALSE

Circle T if the statement is true or F if the statement is false.

T   F   1. One way an application can hide controls from a user is to create them when the program is running, and not display them until they are needed.

T   F   2. An assortment is an object that contains a number of related objects.

T   F   3. Everything in Visual Basic is listed in the Object Browser because everything in Visual Basic is an object.

T   F   4. In a For Each statement, the *group* argument refers to a collection of objects.

T   F   5. In a project containing multiple forms, the statement *This.Close* can be coded in the Exit event procedure for a form to close only that form and not the entire project.

T   F   6. Objects can be added to any collection by coding a statement that uses the collection's *Include()* method.

T   F   7. An application can create separate Controls collections for various objects in the application that should be grouped together.

T   F   8. Adding new controls to an application at run time shows a lack of planning and does nothing to enhance the program.

T   F   9. All collections have an Add() method and a Remove() method.

T   F   10. Unless you specify a name when creating a class module, Visual Basic assigns it the default name of Class1.

T   F   11. The robustness of a program is a measure of its ability to handle unexpected errors without crashing the program.

MULTIPLE CHOICE

Select the best response for the following statements.

1. One way to hide controls on a form until they are needed is to set the control's _____ property to _____.
   a. Enabled, No
   b. Enabled, False
   c. Hide, True
   d. Visible, False
   e. Show, False

2. Which of the following built-in form collections contains each of the controls on a form?
   a. Items
   b. Controls
   c. Objects
   d. Classes
   e. none of the above

3. Which of the following statements is a special statement in Visual Basic used to iterate through a collection?
   a. For Each group
   b. For Each collection
   c. For Each element in group
   d. For Each group element
   e. For Each collection.object

4. Which of the following statements is used with the For Each loop to move from the current object to the next object within the collection?
   a. Next
   b. Loop
   c. DoNext
   d. GetNext
   e. Loop Until

5. When creating a new form or a control when the application program is running, when does the new control become visible to the user?
   a. as soon as it is defined
   b. as soon as it is instantiated
   c. when its Enabled property is set to True
   d. when its visible property is set to True
   e. when the program starts the Show method for the control

6. Which Visual Basic function can be called from an application to run some other existing application?
   a. External()
   b. Shell()
   c. Run()
   d. Execute()
   e. Invoke()

7. Which property of a collection always contains the number of items available in a collection?
   a. Size
   b. Length
   c. Len
   d. Count
   e. Members

8. Which of the following collections would you use to add buttons to or delete buttons from a toolbar while an application is running?
   a. Buttons
   b. Controls
   c. Toolbars
   d. Items
   e. Images

9. Which term refers to a programming technique wherein every time a new control or function is added to a program, the program is tested immediately to make sure the newly added object does not affect the processing of the rest of the program?
   a. Stepwise Development
   b. Incremental Programming
   c. Stepup Refinement
   d. Incidental Testing
   e. Graduated Programming

10. If you accidentally add a class module that you do not need or want in the project, you can delete it in the _____ window.
    a. Solution Explorer
    b. Class Collection
    c. Object Browser
    d. Code window
    e. none of the above

11. Which of the following is a good place to put procedures, functions, and variable declarations that need to be used and accessed by forms and procedures in other parts of the project?
    a. macro
    b. class
    c. module
    d. form
    e. all of the above

12. Which of the properties of a child form is placed into the title bar of the parent form if the child form is maximized?
    a. Caption
    b. (Name)
    c. Title
    d. Text
    e. none of the above

MATCHING

Write the letter of the description in the right column that defines the term in the left column.

_____ 1. element   a. Method used to insert a new object into an existing collection

_____ 2. Shell   b. Collection of objects referenced in a For Each statement

_____ 3. TypeOf   c. A property of a collection

_____ 4. Item   d. Template for an object

_____ 5. Controls   e. Built-in Visual Basic data type that allows a variable to take the value of any control on a form

_____ 6. Count

_____ 7. Add   f. Function that allows one application program to start another application program

_____ 8. Class   g. Used in a conditional statement to determine what kind of object an object is

_____ 9. Group   h. Method used to retrieve a single object from a collection

_____ 10. Control   i. Collection that contains all objects defined on a form

     j. Kind of variable that can point at an object in a For Each statement

FILL IN THE BLANK

Complete the following sentences by writing the correct word or words in the blanks provided.

1. Every control on a form is a part of a(n) _____.

2. An object variable is simply a(n) _____, which contains an address that refers to something in memory.

3. The _____ data type is a built-in data type that allows the variable to take on the value of any control on a given form.

4. It is possible to cause an early exit from a For Each loop by coding a(n) _____ _____ statement in the body of the loop.

5. When using a For Each statement to loop through a collection of objects, you can determine if each object is of a particular type by using an If statement with the _____ keyword.

6. When declaring a collection object, using the keywords _____ _____ instead of *Dim*, creates variables with values that are shared by all forms contained in the application.

7. A form's _____ procedure is executed when the form first loads, which makes it an ideal place to put code to be executed when the application is started.

8. For a collection that you have created, a control can be removed from a form by passing its index value to the collection's _____() method.

9. All collections have a(n) _____() method, which can be used to retrieve a single object from the collection.

10. Creating a hierarchical diagram showing the relationships between classes is one way of depicting an object _____.

11. The _____ definition of an object determines how the various methods and properties of that object are accessible and visible to the programmer.

WRITTEN QUESTIONS

Write a brief answer to the following questions.

1. What is a Visual Basic Controls collection? Explain why it is useful.

2. Describe the purpose and syntax of the For Each statement, and provide an example.

3. Can the For Each statement be used to iterate through a collection looking for only one specific type of control? If so, how is that done? If it can be done, provide an example that iterates through the Controls collection looking only for objects of type Button, and if any are found, it should set their Enabled property to True.

4. Describe the steps involved in creating your own collection.

5. Can a new control be added to a Visual Basic form while a program is running? If so, how is this done?

PROJECT 9-1

One very popular use of computers is to play computer games. In this project, you lay the groundwork for building a computer card game. You create a class to represent one card of a standard 52-card deck, and create a test program to exercise the class. You build on this in the next project and in later lessons.

Begin by creating a user interface with two combo boxes. The first combo box contains the four possible suits (**Hearts**, **Diamonds**, **Clubs**, **Spades**), and the second contains the 13 possible values (**King**, **Queen**, **Jack**, **10, 9, 8, 7, 6, 5, 4, 3, 2, Ace**). When the program starts, the display shows Hearts and King as the default selections. Each of the combo boxes should be appropriately labeled. Next, add two buttons to the test form: **Create Card** and **Exit**. Code the Exit button so that it exits the program when clicked. Save your project as **CardGame1** in a folder named **CardGame1**.

Before you can implement the Create Card button's code, you must create the class that represents a card. Create a class module named **clsCard**. The new class has two properties: Suit and Value, each of which is a string. Make two private variables in the class, strSuit to store the suit of the card and intValue to store the value of the card. The variable strSuit stores the first letter of the suit name, and intValue stores an integer from 1 to 13, inclusive, where 1 represents an Ace, 11 a Jack, 12 a Queen, and 13 a King. All other cards are represented by the number coinciding with their value.

The Get procedure for the property Suit assigns the value in strSuit to the property named Suit. The Set procedure assigns the uppercase form of the first letter of the input string to strSuit. You cannot assume that someone using the program knows how you are representing a card, so you must make sure that the suit is stored properly. Use the string functions and Property procedure skills you have learned from previous lessons and projects to create the class.

The Get procedure for the property Value assigns a string to the Value property. Since the value is represented internally as an integer, you have to use a Select Case statement to determine what string to assign to Value. The value 10 corresponds to the string "10", but all other values assign a single character string to the value. For example,

Case 13: Value = "K"

The Set procedure for the property Value converts an input string to the correct integer value to store in intValue. If the input value is not equal to the string "10", then assign the uppercase form of the first character of the input value to a local variable named strInputValue. Write a Select Case statement that uses the value in strInputValue to assign the correct integer value to intValue. For example,

Case "K": intValue = 13

One additional function must be added that creates and returns a string representation of the card. The code for this function is:

```
Public Function Display() As String
    Display = Value & " " & Suit
End Function
```

Once your class for the card is created, it can be used to implement Create Card. In Create Card's Click event, declare a variable **objCard** of type **clsCard**, and set it equal to a new card. Set the Suit and Value properties of objCard to the values currently in the two combo boxes. Then display a message box with the card value, using the Display method of objCard. Test out all different combinations of suits and values to be sure your class works correctly. When you are sure the class is correct, save your program, and exit Visual Basic.

PROJECT 9-2

The next phase in the development of the card game is to create a class to represent a standard deck of cards that can be shuffled, dealt, and displayed one by one. This program uses the card class developed in the previous application program. To get started, create a folder named **CardGame2** and open a new project also called **CardGame2**. Click the **Project** menu, and then click **Add Existing Item**. When the dialog box opens, locate the **clsCard.vb** class definition in the **CardGame1** folder and select it to be added to the current project.

Next, create the class to represent the deck of cards. The class should be named **clsDeck**. Declare two private variables at the beginning of the class: an array of 52 cards and a short variable to keep track of the next card that can be dealt (use your new clsCard data type). The methods that clsDeck needs are Initialize, Shuffle, DealOneCard, and DisplayCard.

DisplayCard is a function similar to the Display function of the card class created in the previous project. However, this function needs as input the index in the deck's card array of the card to display. Note that the function gets an integer as input and returns the string representation of the card in that position of the deck.

```
Public Function DisplayCard(ByVal intCard As Integer) As String
    DisplayCard = crdDeck(intCard).Display
End Function
```

The Initialize method creates the 52 cards for the deck and puts them into the deck in the order Hearts, Diamonds, Clubs, and Spades, where each suit is ordered Ace, 2, etc., to King. So positions 1 through 13 of the array that holds the cards contain the 13 Hearts once the procedure is done running, positions 14 through 26 hold the Diamonds, and so on. To get this setup correctly, declare two Integer variables in the method, intCounter and intInnerCounter. Below these declarations, use intCounter as the loop control variable in four separate loops. Here is the code for the first loop, where the array holding the cards is named crdDeck:

```
For intCounter = 1 to 13
    crdDeck(intCounter) = New clsCard
    crdDeck(intCounter).Suit ("Hearts") = ""
Next intCounter
```

Write three more loops to assign the correct suits to the remaining 39 cards, following the format of the above code. Once the suits are established, a nested loop like the following, assigns the correct values to each card:

```
For intCounter = 0 to 3
    For intInnerCounter = 1 to 13
        Select Case intInnerCounter
            Case 1: crdDeck (intCounter * 13 + intInnerCounter) .Value ("Ace")
            = ""
            Case 2: crdDeck (intCounter * 13 + intInnerCounter) .Value ("2") =
            ""
            ' Put cases for 3 through Jack here
            Case 12: crdDeck (intCounter * 13 + intInnerCounter)
            .Value("Queen") = ""
            Case 13: crdDeck (intCounter * 13 + intInnerCounter) .Value
            ("King") = ""
        End Select
    Next intInnerCounter
Next intCounter
```

Before you type in this code, make sure you understand how and why it works! The final statement in the Initialize procedure assigns the value of one to the variable intNextCard, maintaining the position of the next card to be dealt.

To test that you have no errors, you must begin work on a simple test application. The test application creates a deck of cards, shuffles the cards, deals cards to two different hands, and resets the deck of cards to standard order, with no cards dealt. Create a form with caption **Test Deck of Cards**. The test form contains three labeled list boxes, one to display the entire deck and one to display each of the two hands of cards. Add a menu named **Deck** to the form. This menu contains three options: **Reset**, **Shuffle**, and **Deal**. Also add a menu with **Exit** as its only member. Code the Exit menu item so it terminates the program.

Now, create a deck of cards by declaring it in the test form's General Declarations section using:

```
Dim objDeck As clsDeck
```

and then create it using the statement:

```
objDeck = New clsDeck
```

in the form's Form_Load procedure. Add code in the Load procedure to call the Reset option. For the random number generator to work correctly, it must also be initialized. Add the statement Randomize at the top of the procedure so this happens as soon as the form is created. Add code so that when the menu option Reset is selected, all the list boxes are cleared, the Initialize method of objDeck is called, and the contents of the deck are displayed to the list box for the deck. Now, run the program. The entire deck in order should be displayed in the deck list. You should also be able to click the Reset option successfully (although the display does not change at this point). If the form displays with no error messages and the cards display in the deck in the proper order, continue coding. If you get any error messages, debug this method and retest the method before continuing.

The Shuffle method of clsDeck uses the random numbers to randomly swap the position of cards in the array. The idea is to use a For loop to walk through the entire array. At each step of the loop, randomly select one of the elements from the current position to the end of the array. Swap the card in the selected position with the card in the current position. The code to implement this idea is:

```
For intCounter = 1 to 52
'pick random position from intCounter to 52, inclusive
    intPosition = (52 - intCounter) * Rnd ( ) + intCounter

    'Swap the cards in intPosition and intCounter
    crdTemp = crdDeck (intCounter)
    crdDeck (intCounter) = crdDeck (intPosition)
    crdDeck (intPosition) = crdTemp
Next intCounter
```

By reading the code, you can determine what variables you must declare in this procedure. After writing the code for the method, call the method from the Shuffle menu option of the test form. After the method has been called, clear the deck list box and display the new order of the deck in its list box. As before, test the method by running the program and selecting Shuffle. Make sure all the cards are displayed, with no repetitions. Also select Reset after shuffling, and be sure the cards reset to the original order. If there are errors, debug them before going on.

The DealOneCard method is a function member of clsDeck, so it returns a value to the calling function. If intNextCard is less than or equal to 52, the value it returns is the next card in the array. Otherwise it outputs an error message. It also increases the value of intNextCard by one when it can return a card, so that the subsequent card is returned on the next call to the method. Here is the code for the body of this method:

```
If intNextCard <= 52 Then
    DealOneCard = crdDeck (intNextCard)
    intNextCard = intNextCard + 1
Else
    MessageBox.Show("No more cards in deck!", "Out of Cards" )
End If
```

This method is used for the Deal menu option. Before implementing the Deal procedure, add variables crdHandl and crdHand2, each arrays of 26 cards, to the General Declarations section of the test form.

When Deal is selected, an input box gets the number of cards to deal to each hand. Do not let the dealing continue if the number is less than 1 or greater than 26. Once the number of cards for each hand is known, one card should be dealt into each hand until the correct number of cards has been dealt. Use a single For loop and deal a card first to one hand, then to the other each time through the loop. After the hands have been dealt, clear their corresponding list boxes and then display the new hands.

Finally, test, test, test! Try the following tests, and then create other tests of your own.

1. Do not shuffle the deck. Deal 26 cards to each hand. Verify that the deck is split in half, with each hand having alternate cards in the deck.

2. Reset and shuffle the deck. Deal five cards to each hand. Check that you get the correct values in each hand (the first 10 cards from the Deck list alternating between the two Hand lists). Without resetting the deck, deal five more cards to each hand. The hands now contain the next 10 cards in the deck, since the index in the deck of cards did not move from the last time you dealt cards.

3. Reset and shuffle again. Deal seven cards to each hand. Without resetting the deck, click the Deal option again. This time specify 26 cards for each hand. You do not get repeated message box messages that the deck is out of cards. How can you fix this? Use the debugging skills you have learned along with your knowledge of Visual Basic to fix the problem. (*Hint*: It can be easily fixed in the mnuDeckDeal_Click procedure, but be sure you fix the entire problem, not just a portion of it.) When you think you have this bug fixed, be sure to run the same test again to make certain that fixing one aspect of the problem did not create another.

When you are satisfied that your classes and your test program are performing as expected, close the project. You will be using these two classes in another project later.

UNIT 2 REVIEW

TRUE/FALSE

Circle T if the statement is true or F if the statement is false.

T   F   **1.** In break mode, the Step Out command can be used to finish the execution of the current procedure without single-stepping, and pass control to the statement that follows the current procedure.

T   F   **2.** A value of one (1) is returned to the program when a user clicks an OK button in the message box dialog box.

T   F   **3.** The Error Instruction Pointer is a yellow arrow that appears in the left margin of the Code window when break mode is entered as the result of a run-time error.

T   F   **4.** The Wrappable property of a TextBox control determines if text wraps to the next line when needed.

T   F   **5.** Code that can be used in more than one program is called reentrant code.

T   F   **6.** In a For Each loop, the Next statement moves *element* from the current object in the group to the next object in the group.

T   F   **7.** You connect a DataGrid control to a dataset by setting its DataSetName property to the name defined for the dataset.

T   F   **8.** Visual Basic does not allow a toolbar to be modified once a program begins executing.

T   F   **9.** When resizing an array, Visual Basic automatically copies any data from the current array to the new array.

T   F **10.** The process of rerouting program flow to process run-time errors that may occur is called error trapping.

T   F **11.** If the user clicks the Cancel button in a message box, a value of two (2) is returned to the program.

T   F **12.** The Finally portion of a Try-Catch-Finally statement is required.

T   F **13.** The UBound() function is used to determine how many items are contained in an existing array.

T   F **14.** ODBC is just one example of an API.

T   F **15.** Every control on every Visual Basic form is a part of a collection.

T   F **16.** You can connect a database field to an individual text box using the Text property of the text box.

T   F **17.** The icons used for a toolbar are stored in a ToolbarIcon control.

T   F **18.** One feature of Visual Basic that makes it so powerful and attractive to programmers is the ability to add controls to a form while a program is executing.

T   F **19.** A record is the smallest unit of information about an object in a database table.

T   F **20.** Visual Basic has a built-in constant named Nil that is used to represent an empty object.

MULTIPLE CHOICE

Select the best response for the following statements.

1. What is the maximum number of buttons that can be displayed in a MessageBox control?
   - **a.** 1
   - **b.** 2
   - **c.** 3
   - **d.** 4
   - **e.** 5

2. What happens if you use the On Error Resume Next statement in a program and a run-time error occurs when the program executes?
   - **a.** A dialog box appears asking if you want to enter break mode.
   - **b.** The program crashes instantly.
   - **c.** Visual Basic automatically enters break mode.
   - **d.** A warning message appears, and the program resumes execution when the user clicks OK in the message box.
   - **e.** Nothing happens; the error is ignored, no message is generated, and the program continues.

3. Which keyword can be used in a For Each loop in conjunction with an If statement to determine what type of control is being examined?
   - **a.** TypeIs
   - **b.** TypeOf
   - **c.** WhenType
   - **d.** IfType
   - **e.** ForType

4. Which of the following database engines does Microsoft Access use?
   - **a.** Microsoft Jet
   - **b.** Microsoft OLE DB Provider for ODBC
   - **c.** SQL Driver
   - **d.** Microsoft DB Engine
   - **e.** none of the above

5. What is the maximum number of characters that can be returned from an InputBox function?
   - **a.** 31
   - **b.** 63
   - **c.** 127
   - **d.** 255
   - **e.** 511

6. Which of the following statements allows you to terminate the processing of a For Each loop before reaching the end of the collection?
   - **a.** For Each Exit
   - **b.** For Exit
   - **c.** Quit
   - **d.** Exit Loop
   - **e.** Exit For

7. The SQL _____ statement is used to retrieve data from a database.
   - **a.** Retrieve
   - **b.** Select
   - **c.** Request
   - **d.** Read
   - **e.** Get

8. Which command in an event procedure parameter list ensures that the code in the procedure cannot change the value of the variable passed as a parameter?
   - **a.** Private
   - **b.** ByParm
   - **c.** ByVal
   - **d.** Local
   - **e.** none of the above

9. Which keyword is used in a program to fire off an event handler when the event is triggered?
   - **a.** WithEvent
   - **b.** CallEvent
   - **c.** ProcessEvent
   - **d.** RaiseEvent
   - **e.** DoEvent

10. Which of the following would you use to set a conditional breakpoint in a Visual Basic application?
- **a.** Watch window
- **b.** Object window
- **c.** Command window
- **d.** Breakpoint Condition dialog box
- **e.** Breakpoint dialog box

11. Which File object method is used to create a new text file?
- **a.** CreateFile
- **b.** CreateText
- **c.** NewFile
- **d.** OpenFile
- **e.** OpenText

12. Which statement do you use to close the window that currently has the focus without terminating the entire application?
- **a.** Close(This)
- **b.** Close(Me)
- **c.** Me.Close
- **d.** This.Close
- **e.** none of the above

13. Which of the following is maintained by the Visual Basic system and contains information about any recent errors?
- **a.** Err object
- **b.** Error object
- **c.** error log
- **d.** Watch window
- **e.** RecentError object

14. Which panel of the Visual Basic Toolbox contains the OleDbDataAdapter control?
- **a.** General
- **b.** Components
- **c.** Windows Forms
- **d.** Data
- **e.** Database

15. _____ means that the same method or property may have different meanings when connected to different objects.
- **a.** Reusability
- **b.** Inheritance
- **c.** Encapsulation
- **d.** Redundancy
- **e.** Polymorphism

16. When creating an event handler for a class, which of the following statements could be coded in the calling program to declare an object variable for the event?
- **a.** Dim ForEvents MyCar As clsAuto
- **b.** Dim WithEvents MyCar As clsAuto
- **c.** Dim WhenEvents MyCar As clsAuto
- **d.** Dim IfEvents MyCar As clsAuto
- **e.** Dim ThisEvents MyCar As clsAuto

17. Typing the statement Select End at the end of the Select Case block instead of typing End Select is an example of what type of error?
- **a.** run-time
- **b.** syntax
- **c.** precompile
- **d.** Option Explicit violation
- **e.** Option Strict violation

18 Which of the following terms defines an object that contains a number of related objects?
- **a.** Set
- **b.** List
- **c.** Collection
- **d.** Group
- **e.** Class

19. Which of the following keywords is used to create a user-defined data type?
- **a.** UDT
- **b.** Record
- **c.** Build
- **d.** UDTType
- **e.** Structure

20. Which of the following keywords can be used with the ReDim command to retain the current set of data when an array is resized?
    a. Keep
    b. Copy
    c. Preserve
    d. Retain
    e. Save

FILL IN THE BLANK

Complete the following sentences by writing the correct word or words in the blanks provided.

1. The message box dialog box is _____, which means that program processing is suspended until the user responds to the dialog box.

2. When coding a Try-Catch-Finally statement, there may be more than one _____ section coded.

3. The most important property of a connection object is the _____, which provides the information necessary to access a database.

4. All of the controls on a Visual Basic form are contained in the _____ collection.

5. A(n) _____ is an organized collection of related data.

6. When reading database records, the _____ property of the CurrencyManager object can be used to determine the current location within the database.

7. When a user clicks the Cancel button in an input box dialog box, a(n) _____ string is returned to the program.

8. When you are in Immediate mode, you can return to Command mode by entering the command _____.

9. The _____ property of a toolbar object is used to bind the edges of a toolbar control to a particular edge of the container.

10. The _____ Browser allows you to examine classes and the properties of the objects created from those classes.

11. The _____ function can be used, along with its built-in constants, to format a string in a particular fashion.

12. Leading spaces at the beginning of a string, and trailing spaces at the end of string, can be removed by using the _____ function.

13. When creating a database connection to an Access database, you can use the _____ Builder to add the tables, fields, and SQL statements necessary to access the data.

14. You can insert a new object into a collection using the _____() method of the collection object.

15. A very simple class very closely resembles a(n) _____.

16. Watch expressions are set in the _____ dialog box.

17. You can run some other program from within an executing application by using the _____() function.

18. When a user enters input from a keyboard, the keyboard produces a(n) _____ character for each key that is pressed.

19. Converting a variable of type Integer to a variable of type Decimal is one example of a(n) _____ conversion.

20. In the syntax of the For Each statement, the _____ is usually the kind of variable that can point at an object in the collection being processed.

Unit 3: Creating and Using New Controls

LESSON 10   **USING SPECIAL CONTROLS TO ENHANCE THE USER INTERFACE**

LESSON 11   **BUILDING AND USING A USER CONTROL**

UNIT 3 REVIEW

LESSON 10   USING SPECIAL CONTROLS TO ENHANCE THE USER INTERFACE

TRUE/FALSE

Circle T if the statement is true or F if the statement is false.

T   F   1. A picture box can be stretched or shrunk to fit an image contained within the PictureBox control.

T   F   2. Clicking on a trackbar is equivalent to pressing the Page Up and Page Down keys on the keyboard.

T   F   3. The MarkFrequency property of the TrackBar control determines the value of each mark displayed on the control's scale.

T   F   4. The images associated with an ImageList control must be added to the control at design time.

T   F   5. For an image list named MyImageList, the programming code statement, *x = MyImageList. Images.Count*, could be coded to determine how many images are currently in the collection.

T   F   6. The trackbar thumb can be moved along the scale by pressing the left or right arrow keys, the Page Up and Page Down keys, or by clicking and dragging it with the mouse.

T   F   7. A StatusBar control typically contains only one panel.

T   F   8. Most programmers clearly remember the details of the code they write and don't usually need to create detailed documentation of the program.

T   F   9. In discussing hierarchical structures, the family metaphor uses the terms parents, children, and siblings to describe relationships among items in a tree.

T   F   10. In family metaphor terminology, two items that have the same parent are called twins.

T   F   11. Tree processing in Visual Basic makes use of recursive functions, which are functions that call themselves.

T   F   12. A ProgressBar control is frequently used in programs to inform the user about the progress of some long-running operation or process.

T   F   13. When a new node is added to a tree structure, a pointer to the node's parent node is automatically set in the new node's DescendentOf property.

T   F   14. A tab page created in a Visual Basic application is another type of container.

T   F   15. The ChangeBy property determines the amount that a value displayed in a NumericUpDown control changes when one of the arrows is clicked.

MULTIPLE CHOICE

Select the best response for the following statements.

1. Which Visual Basic control is used as the source of images to be used in a PictureBox control?
   a. PictureList
   b. ImageList
   c. PictureBoxList
   d. PictureSet
   e. ImageSet

2. Which of the following trackbar properties is used to specify the upper and lower bounds of the control's range?
   a. Upper, Lower
   b. High, Low
   c. Left, Right
   d. Maximum, Minimum
   e. Start, Stop

3. Which trackbar property below determines how far the thumb moves when the user presses the left or right arrow key?
   a. ArrowChange
   b. RangeChange
   c. SmallChange
   d. LargeChange
   e. ClickChange

4. Which PictureBox control property/value pair below would you set to cause an image contained in a PictureBox control to expand itself or shrink itself to fit the size of the control?
   a. AutoSize/True
   b. SizeMode/StretchImage
   c. AutoFit/Yes
   d. SizeType/SizeToFit
   e. FillMode/Stretch

5. Which method is part of the Image type, and can be used to identify a specific image stored on a disk or other medium, such as a CD.
   a. FromFile
   b. InFile
   c. OfFile
   d. WithFile
   e. GetFile

6. Which of the following is *not* a view option that can be referenced using a ListView control?
   a. Large Icons
   b. Small Icons
   c. Details
   d. List
   e. Summary

7. Which property of the StatusBar control would you use to change its position on the form?
   a. Anchor
   b. Location
   c. Dock
   d. Edge
   e. Side

8. Which term is commonly used in program documentation to describe the status and values of parameters after a function or procedure has finished executing?
   a. exit status
   b. exit-conditions
   c. post-execution status
   d. post-conditions
   e. none of the above

9. Which term is used in the tree metaphor when referring to an item in a tree structure that has no branches?
   a. leaf
   b. orphan
   c. sibling
   d. terminator
   e. child

10. Every item in a tree is a programmable object that belongs to which of the following Visual Basic collections?
    a. Items
    b. TreeNode
    c. Tree
    d. TreeItem
    e. Nodes

11. Which property of the TreeView control contains a pointer to the first item in the tree?
    a. RootNode
    b. TopNode
    c. FirstNode
    d. Top
    e. Start

12. When a user selects an item from a TreeView control, which event handler procedure is passed a pointer to the node?
    a. Click
    b. Selected
    c. AfterSelect
    d. NodeSelect
    e. NodeClick

13. What happens if a node that has children is removed from the tree?
    a. All children of that node are lost.
    b. All children are linked to the parent of the removed node.
    c. All children are linked to a sibling of the removed node.
    d. All children of the removed node are used to create a new and separate tree.
    e. The children are linked to an empty node.

14. Which property of the NumericUpDown control contains the current and displayed value of the control?
    a. Text
    b. Current
    c. Value
    d. Caption
    e. Number

15. Which control allows a user to enter dates and times into a program?
    a. TimePicker
    b. DateTimePicker
    c. DatePicker
    d. both a and c
    e. a, b, and c

MATCHING

Write the letter of the description in the right column that defines the term in the left column.

_____ 1. SmallChange

_____ 2. View

_____ 3. Value

_____ 4. Parent

_____ 5. Text

_____ 6. SizeMode

_____ 7. sibling

_____ 8. LargeChange

_____ 9. leaf

_____ 10. root

a. Node in a tree that has the same parent as a node adjacent to it on the same level

b. Property of a trackbar that determines how far the thumb moves if the mouse is clicked on the trackbar next to the thumb

c. Item in a tree that has no branches

d. Top-level item in a tree structure

e. Property of a trackbar that determines how far the thumb moves when an arrow key is pressed

f. Property of a ListView control that determines how information is formatted

g. Property of a status bar panel that determines what is displayed in that panel

h. Property of a trackbar that indicates the current position of the thumb

i. Property of a tree node that points to the node from which the current node is descended

j. Property of a PictureBox control used to control images placed in the control

FILL IN THE BLANK

Complete the following sentences by writing the correct word or words in the blanks provided.

1. A TrackBar control consists of a thumb, which can be moved with the mouse, and _____ marks that indicate the current position within a range of values.

2. The current position of the TrackBar thumb can be determined by examining the control's _____ property.

3. When entering program code for an application, remember that the proper use of _____ space can make your code much easier to read and follow.

4. For each image in an ImageList control's Images collection, the value of each image's _____ property reflects the order in which the image was added to the collection.

5. Variables defined in an event procedure are reinitialized every time the procedure is executed unless they are declared using the _____ keyword.

6. Windows Explorer is one example of an application that uses a(n) _____ control to display and examine disk drives and folders.

7. The current time and the icons for background tasks are usually displayed in a panel on the _____ side of the status bar.

8. A program can access a status bar panel using the Index property of the _____ collection.

9. Using a tree metaphor, the first item in the hierarchy of the tree is called the _____.

10. In either tree or family metaphor terminology, every item in a tree structure is called a(n) _____.

11. When searching a tree for a particular item, the recursive function _____ can be called to recursively process the tree until the item is found or all items have been searched.

12. The ProgressBar control has _____ and _____ properties that define the range of the bar.

13. When searching a node for some string value, the _____ function can be used to locate the desired string in the Text property of the node being examined.

14. Tab pages can be created in Visual Basic programs by accessing the _____ tool in the Toolbox.

15. The methods used to change the value displayed by a NumericUpDown control when one of the arrows is clicked are the _____ and _____ methods.

WRITTEN QUESTIONS

Write a brief answer to the following questions.

1. What is the purpose of the TrackBar control? Describe the major components of a trackbar.

2. Describe the purpose of the following TrackBar control properties: Value, Minimum, Maximum, SmallChange, and LargeChange.

3. Which property of the PictureBox control can be set to StretchImage? What is the effect of setting that property to that value?

4. Name and describe the four views available for the ListView control.

5. Provide a brief description of the StatusBar control.

6. Using the family metaphor, give a short description of a tree. Name the various items that make up a tree, and indicate their relationship to each other.

7. What is a Visual Basic TabControl?

8. Describe the appearance and function of a NumericUpDown control. Provide an example of where you may see this type of control.

9. Explain the concept of white space and how it can enhance a Visual Basic program.

10. What types of information are included in program documentation?

11. What is a TreeView control? Describe some of its properties and its use.

PROJECT 10-1

In this program, you return to the medical records program you have worked on in previous lessons. Copy the contents of the **MedicalRecords5** folder that you created in the Lesson 8 Programming at Work exercise into a folder named **MedicalRecords6**. You make your changes in the new folder to preserve the old program.

In this application, you convert the structure named PatientData to a class named clsPatientData. Add a class module to the program and name it **clsPatientData.** Declare the same fields as are currently defined in the existing structure. Declare all of them as Public, which makes this a very small and easy class to create. Use the same names for each instance variable to minimize the amount of code that needs to be changed in the program. Delete the structure from the form code window. In the event procedure for the Load button of the form, you need to add a line to create an instance of each object as they are added to the array. Do that, and run the program. The program should run as it did before. Save your changes, and exit the program when done.

PROJECT 10-2

In this project, you convert the medical records program into a multiform (but not an MDI) application. You create a front-end form that users see or when they start the program. You also modify the existing form by hiding some controls and removing or renaming others. Copy the contents of the **MedicalRecords6** folder to a new folder named **MedicalRecords7**, and make your changes in that folder. Open the project, and create a new form. Name the form **PatDbMain**. Change the Text property to **Medical Record Database Main Form**. Add six labels to the form, and five command buttons. One label should be positioned near the top of the form, and its Text property should read **Please select one of the following options**. Position the five command buttons on the right edge of the form, one on top of the other so they run down the right edge of the form. The button names should be, from top to bottom, **btnOpen, btnSave, btnBrowse, btnUpdate, btnExit**. The Text properties should be changed to read, again from top to bottom, **&Open, &Save, &Browse, &Update**, and **E&xit**. Position the remaining five labels to the left of each button, and change their Text property to some message that reflects the purpose of each button.

Click the project name (**Medical Records**) in the Solution Explorer, and then right-click the name to display the shortcut menu. Click the **Properties** option. Click the list arrow for the **Startup Object** combo box field, and select the **PatDbMain** form as the startup form. Close the dialog box.

Add a module to the project that will be used to declare the global variables needed in a multiform project. Name the module **modPatientDb.** Open the Code window for the frmPatientInfoEntry form. Cut the variables in the Declarations section of that form and paste them into the new module you just added. Add the word **Public** to the Const declaration line, and change the Dim statement for the remaining constants to the word **Public** so they can be accessed from outside the module. Add another Boolean variable named **DoUpdate.**

Delete the **OpenFileDialog** and **SaveFileDialog** controls from the frmPatientInfoEntry form. The responsibility for opening the file and loading the array, and saving and closing the file is moved to the PatDbMain form. Locate the code for opening and closing the files and move it to the event procedures for the Open and Save buttons in PatDbMain. Add an **OpenFileDialog** and a **SaveFileDialog** control to the PatDbMain form. Any code in frmPatientInfoEntry that checks the DbLoaded variable (or whatever name you used in your program) should also be moved to the PatDbMain form. That form now assumes the responsibility for forcing the user to load a data file before they can perform any other operations, except exiting the program.

Write the code for the Browse button so that it declares a new copy of the PatientInfoEntry form, similar to the way you declared a new copy of an MDI form. It must also check to be sure a database has been loaded. If not, display a message and exit the event procedure. If the database has been loaded, set the DoUpdate variable to a value of False, and display the frmPatientInfoEntry form. The event procedure for the Update button is similar, except it sets the DoUpdate variable to True.

In the event procedure for the Exit button, insert the line **Application.Exit().** In the Load event procedure for the PatDbMain form, move the statements from the frmPatientInfoEntry form Load procedure that initialize the LastPatient, CurPatient, and the path name variables. Leave the code that loads the combo boxes in the PatientInfoEntry form Load procedure.

Display the frmPatientInfoEntry form. Change the text on the buttons that currently read *Load File* and *Save File* to **Add Record** and **Delete Record.** Change the button names to **btnAdd** and **btnDelete.** Change the button that reads *Exit* to read **Return to Main Form.** Change the event procedure for that button to execute the line Me.Close() to unload the form. Locate the Load procedure for the frmPatientInfoEntry form. Following the code that initializes the combo boxes, insert the code statement that initializes the total number of records in the array text box. When this form is "shown" by the PatDbMain form, the array has been loaded but no records are yet visible in the text boxes. Set the CurPatient variable to a value of the **LastPatient - 1,** which causes the Next button event procedure to "wrap" the array and show the first record. The Load procedure must also check the DoUpdate variable. If it is False, the Add Record and the Delete Record buttons should be made invisible so the user cannot access the update routines. Finally, it should call the btnNext_Click event procedure to display the first record.

Select **btnAdd** from the Class Name list box, and Click from the Method Name list box. When a new record is to be added, this event procedure must check to be sure the array is not full. If there is room in the array, the new record is added to the end of the array. Set the **CurPatient** variable equal to LastPatient, and the LastPatient variable is incremented by one. Create a new patient object using the CurPatient variable as the index of the array, and move the fields from the text boxes to the array entry. Update the total records text box on the form, and display the index of the current record (relative to one) in the current record text box.

Select **btnDelete** from the Class Name list box, and Click from the Method Name list box. The first thing this procedure needs to do is verify that the user really wants to delete the current record. Use an input box or a message box to obtain some response from the user to verify the deletion. Once confirmed, if the current record is not the last record in the array, copy the contents from the last location (last filled location) to the current location in the array. If the record being deleted is the last record in the array, just decrement the CurPatient variable to point at the previous record. In either case, decrement the LastPatient variable to indicate one less record in the array, update the total record count text box, and call the btnNext_Click procedure to display the next record in the array.

Save your changes, and build and run the project. Test all buttons and operations completely. Test extreme conditions to see if you can cause the program to fail. Fix any errors you find, and test the program again. When you are satisfied the program is working correctly, save it and exit Visual Basic.

PROGRAMMING AT WORK

The Medical Records database program has gained a lot of functionality since you created it. It is close to becoming a full-fledged application. However, it still has a number of deficiencies or problems that need to be addressed. In this project, you polish it up a bit and work on making it a more robust program. Copy the contents of the **MedicalRecords7** folder to a new folder named **MedicalRecords8**. Make all of your changes in this folder. Using the Visual Basic skills you have learned to this point, perform the following operations on the program.

1. The program does not currently allow the user to create a new database file, other than saving the existing file using a different name. Modify the program so the user can elect to create a brand new file (add a **New** button to PatDbMain and add associated code where needed) if they so desire. When this option is selected, the New button's Click procedure should cause the frmPatientInfoEntry form to be displayed with all buttons visible. This procedure should set the LastPatient variable to a value of zero to indicate there is nothing currently in the array. Once the patient entry form has been displayed, if the user does actually add records to the array and control is returned to the PatDbMain form, the program must warn the user if they attempt to exit the program without saving the new data in a file.

2. The program does not currently check to see if the user updates a record that is displayed on the form. The user could change anything in the form, and click the Next or Previous button and the program would not currently update the array to reflect those changes. Add this functionality to the program. You can add an Update button that the user must click to update a record, or you can just compare the contents of the form fields with the array fields every time the user clicks the Next or Previous button. You decide how best to handle this situation.

3. The toolbar has been neglected for the last several changes to the program. Update the toolbar buttons and event procedures to reflect the current operation of the program. As with the Add Record, Update Record, Clear Fields, and Delete Record command buttons, when you add equivalent buttons to the toolbar, they should also be invisible when in Browse mode.

4. With the command buttons and the toolbar buttons in place, the menu is not needed anymore. Delete any remaining traces of menu code or controls that may remain in the program.

5. What happens if the user clicks the Clear Fields button and then clicks the Add Record button? The program does not currently check to ensure there is data in the form text fields before adding an object to the array. Add whatever code is necessary to make certain that at least some of the fields contain valid data before creating a new object. You decide which fields are required. What happens if the user does the same thing with the Clear Fields and the Delete Record buttons? Add code to prevent an error in that case also. (*Hint*: The btnClear_Click event procedure currently only clears the text box fields. It does not reset the current record pointer. You may need to make modifications there before deciding what to do in the add and delete routines. There are several ways to handle this operation. Use your judgment to arrive at a workable solution.) This same type of check needs to be made for the Update Record procedure as well.

6. Add a Help form to the program. Add a button on the PatientInfoEntry form that the user can click to get some basic instructions on how to add a record, how to delete a record, and how to update a record. Create several labels on the form that make it easy for the user to understand what steps they need to take for each of those operations. Create the code necessary to create an instance of the form and to display it when the button is clicked. (*Note*: Just as the update buttons are invisible when the user is in Browse mode, the Help button can be made invisible as well until the user enters Update mode.)

7. Set the tab order for the PatientInfoEntry form so the user can press the Tab key and move through the text fields in order. Make certain the record count and the current record text boxes are inaccessible to the user yet still display their respective data values.

8. And finally, there is nothing currently in place to prevent the user from just clicking the Add Record button repeatedly, without actually entering new data. The user could add five, ten, or more copies of the same exact record. Add code to the Add event procedure to examine the ID Number field for a record being added, and compare it to existing objects in the array. If that ID Number is already there, do not process the add, but give the user an error message, and let them try again. All patients must have a unique ID number, at the very least.

Be sure you completely test all of your changes, and correct any errors you may find. You want to make your program as foolproof as you can. Of course, there are still areas of error checking and trapping that have not been implemented for this project yet. But, you want it to be very solid under normal working circumstances.

LESSON 11   BUILDING AND USING A USER CONTROL

TRUE/FALSE

Circle T if the statement is true or F if the statement is false.

T   F   1. Creating a user control to package commonly used functions can help a programmer to achieve consistent performance across multiple applications.

T   F   2. One way to create a user control is to enhance an existing control to give it added functionality.

T   F   3. You can add a user control to a Visual Basic application by selecting the Add User Control option from the Tools menu.

T   F   4. To view the Code window for a user control, you can click the View Code button in the Control Explorer window.

T   F   5. To add a user control to a form for testing, you must first close the user control's Designer window.

T   F   6. A user control is really nothing more than a class definition, so the rules for creating properties for a control are the same as for a class.

T   F   7. As with other Visual Basic controls, user controls can be viewed in the Object Browser.

T   F   8. Any user control variable that is declared in the Declarations section of the control is visible to and accessible by the application.

T   F   9. A Window Control Library project is similar to a standard Visual Basic application project and can be run and tested using the commands on the Debug menu.

T   F   10. In many companies that design and create application or system software programs, formal code walk-throughs are held to examine current development projects and look for bugs or design flaws before the program is completed.

T   F   11. When you are not adding controls to a form or other container, you can get more display room on your screen by clicking the Close button on the Toolbox to close it.

T   F   12. When creating a new user control from an existing user control, it is often necessary to modify the original control from within the inherited control.

T   F   13. When an existing user control is added to a new project and it is viewed in the Designer window of the new project, the controls for the user control are grayed out to indicate they cannot be modified.

T   F   14. Visual Basic allows you to create user-drawn controls, which let you define the appearance of the user interface.

T   F   15. In Visual Basic, a FillBrush object is used to fill graphic shapes, such as rectangles or polygons, with some specified color.

MULTIPLE CHOICE

Select the best response for the following statements.

1. Which of the following methods can be used to create a user control?
   a. Combine existing controls and write code to bind them together.
   b. Draw an original control to provide a new user interface.
   c. Use the Visual Basic User Control Wizard.
   d. both a and b
   e. a, b, and c

2. Which of the following Visual Basic controls has no visible presence as far as the user interface goes?
   a. PictureBox
   b. ImageList
   c. StatusBar
   d. TrackBar
   e. none of the above

3. The User Control icon is found in the Templates window of which of the following dialog boxes?
   a. Add User Control
   b. Add Control
   c. Add New Item
   d. Add New Object
   e. Add Object

4. Verifying by hand the output computations required for a user control is
   a. a waste of time.
   b. a good idea if you have the time to do it.
   c. a task usually performed by the software testing group.
   d. an essential part of program testing.
   e. not really necessary with modern software.

5. When a user control's Designer window is open,
   a. the control's icon is grayed out in the Toolbox.
   b. the control cannot be added to a project.
   c. the control cannot be used in an existing application containing the control.
   d. both a and b
   e. a, b, and c

6. When you create a user control, you actually create
   a. a template for creating as many of these controls as you want.
   b. a class definition.
   c. a private object to which the user has no access.
   d. both a and b
   e. none of the above

7. Variables of a user control may not be visible using the Object Browser if they were
   a. declared in the Declarations section using the _Private_ keyword.
   b. declared in the Declarations section using the _Hidden_ keyword.
   c. declared in a Click event handler of the control.
   d. declared in the Declarations section using the _Dim_ keyword.
   e. none of the above—all variables of a user control are always visible.

8. In order to use a user control created for one application in other applications, which of the following steps must be performed?
   a. In the new application, click the Project menu, choose Add Existing Item, and locate the user control.
   b. In the new application, click the File menu, choose Add Existing Item, and locate the user control.
   c. You cannot use a user control in any application other than the one for which it was created.
   d. In the new application, click the Project menu, choose Add User Control, and locate the user control.
   e. You must create a Windows Control Project library, and add the control to that project.

9. Which user control property stores additional data about the control, and is frequently used to distinguish the control from other controls?
   a. Name
   b. Tag
   c. ContextMenu
   d. Appearance
   e. Status

10. Files that contain supporting information needed to run a user control are called DLLs, which stands for which of the following?
    a. Database Load Library
    b. Dynamic Load Library
    c. Distributed Link Library
    d. Dynamic Link Library
    e. Dynamic Lookup Library

11. The first computer spreadsheet program, created in 1979, was called
    a. Excel.
    b. Quattro Pro.
    c. Visicalc.
    d. Quicken.
    e. Lotus123.

12. If an existing user control is added to a Windows Control Library project, when viewed in the Code window, the line immediately below the Public Class statement begins with which of the following statements?
    a. Inherits
    b. SubClass
    c. InheritsFrom
    d. DescendentOf
    e. RelatedTo

13. Which dialog box would you use to select particular components from a Windows Library Project to be added to the current project?
    a. Component Picker
    b. ControlComponent Picker
    c. Inheritance Picker
    d. UserControl Picker
    e. Library Picker

14. Which of the following is a library of classes within Visual Basic that can be used to draw graphic images and create graphic objects?
    a. System.Shapes
    b. System.Paint
    c. Graphics.Tools
    d. Graphics.Paint
    e. System.Drawing

15. Which Graphics class method would be used to display text on the face of some graphic control?
    a. DrawText
    b. DrawString
    c. PaintText
    d. TextDraw
    e. TextPaint

16. In the statement *e.Graphics.DrawRectangle(usePen, e.ClipRectangle)*, what is the purpose of the usePen parameter?

    a. It specifies that the rectangle must be drawn using a pen object.

    b. It specifies the object used to fill the interior of the rectangle with the currently selected color.

    c. It indicates the name of an object to place inside the rectangle.

    d. It contains the specifications for the width and the color of the rectangle.

    e. none of the above

17. Which of the following steps must you take in order to draw text on a control?

    a. Create an object representing the font.

    b. Declare a font object as Public.

    c. Call the DrawText method to paint the text.

    d. both a and b

    e. both a and c

MATCHING

Write the letter of the description in the right column that defines the term in the left column.

_____ **1.** Location

_____ **2.** Fixed3D

_____ **3.** Font

_____ **4.** Locked

_____ **5.** Pen

_____ **6.** DrawString

_____ **7.** Windows Control Library

_____ **8.** Tag

_____ **9.** Paint

_____ **10.** Appearance

a. User control property that stores additional information about the control

b. Type of project that allows you to add user controls to it

c. User control property that defines where the control appears

d. User-drawn control's event procedure that builds the visual appearance of the control

e. Graphics class object used to draw on a control

f. Type of object required to draw text on a control

g. User control property that can be set to 3-D or flat

h. Graphics class method used to draw text on a user-drawn control

i. User control property that determines if the control can be moved

j. One possible border style for a control

FILL IN THE BLANK

Complete the following sentences by writing the correct word or words in the blanks provided.

1. User controls can be added to the Visual Basic _____, and then added to an application.

2. A control that has no _____ presence gives the program the most flexibility, and also requires the programmer to do the most work.

3. When a new user control is created, it appears in its own Designer, and it resembles a standard Windows form except it has no _____.

4. A user control cannot be started like an application; it must first be _____, and then _____ to the application.

5. When a user control has an error in it, you can reopen its Designer to fix the error, but the changes do not take effect until the control is _____.

6. Any user control's variables declared in the _____ section of the control are available to the application program as properties if they were declared with the _____ keyword.

7. When viewing a user control's variable in the Object Browser, if the variable is not available to the application using the control, the symbol of a(n) _____ appears next to the variable name.

8. When you open a Windows Control Library project, it automatically opens a new _____ control.

9. The _____ property of the user control determines where the control is placed relative to the upper-left corner of its container.

10. You can add a DLL to a project by right-clicking _____ in the Solution Explorer, and then selecting Add References to open that dialog box.

11. When a new Windows Control Library project is created, there is a default control named _____ that is automatically created when the project starts and can be deleted from the Solution Explorer window.

12. If you open the Object Browser, you see that the UserControl class is derived from the _____ class.

13. The use of _____ controls ensures that the existing functions of the original control are not changed, and also ensures that important functions are used consistently without being modified.

14. Unlike a regular user control, a user-drawn control uses no standard parts out of the _____.

15. Every time a property of a user-drawn control is changed, you should call the control's _____ event to redraw the control.

PROJECT 11-1

In this program, you create a user control to calculate a sales tax on a subtotal, and then add the two to produce a grand total. Start a new Visual Basic project and save it as **SalesTaxTest** in a folder named **SalesTaxTest**. Change the Text property of the form to read **Test Sales Tax Control**. Add a user control to the project. Name the user control **SalesTax**. Place six labels on the user control form, and one button. Position three of the labels on the left side of the form, one on top of the other, and position the other three labels on the right side of the form, each one opposite one of the labels on the left side. Change the Text properties of the three leftmost labels to **Subtotal:**, **Tax at 6%:**, and **Grand Total:**.

Name the three rightmost labels, from top to bottom, **lblSubtotal**, **lblTax**, and **lblGrandTotal**, and clear the Text property for these labels. Set the BackColor to **White**, and change the border style to **Fixed3D.** Format the font type and size for all labels as you wish. Position the button at the bottom of the form, name it **btnCalculate**, and set the Text to read **Calculate Tax and Total**. Write the code so the user control multiplies the value in the Subtotal label by a constant value of 6%, and stores the result in the Grand Total label. Format the Grand Total field so it displays two decimal places. Build the user control when all code has been entered, and close the form for the control so it is available in the Toolbox.

Add the user control **SalesTax** to the form for the test project, and position it in the lower-right corner of the form. Add three more labels, and three text boxes to the test form. Stack the three text boxes above the user control's rightmost labels. Position the label controls above the user control's leftmost labels, one each opposite one of the text boxes. Name the top text box **txtName**, the middle text box **txtQty**, and the last text box **txtPrice**. Clear the Text property for all text boxes. Change the Text properties for the labels to read, **Item Name:**, **Item Qty:**, and **Item Price:**. Add three command buttons to the form, anywhere you want to place them. Name one of them **btnPurchase**, and change its Text property to **Purchase Item**. Name the other one **btnClear**, and change its Text property to **Clear Fields**. Name the last one **btnExit**, and change its Text property to **Exit**. Enter code for the Exit button to end the application. Enter code for the Purchase button to verify that a numeric quantity and price have been entered for an item, multiply the price times the quantity, and then add the result to the value in the Subtotal field of the user control. If the user clicks the Clear button, clear all fields and allow the user to enter a new item. When all items are entered, click the Calculate button on the user control to multiply the subtotal times the tax rate and display a grand total value. Test the project and make any corrections to the project or the user control that are required. Save your changes and exit Visual Basic.

PROJECT 11-2

Create a Windows Control Library project named **SalesTaxDLL** and save it in a folder of that name. Delete the default user control, add the **SalesTax.vb** user control you created in Project 11-1 to the control project, and build the solution to create a **SalesTaxDLL.dll** file. Close the project.

Create a new windows application project named **EnterOrder** and save it in a folder of the same name. Add a reference to the project of the SalesTaxDLL file you just created. Add the **SalesTax.vb** form to the project and build the solution to add the control to the Toolbox. Add the user control to the project form. Add a list box to the form, and add two buttons to the form. One button is used to add an item to an order, and the other button is used to exit the program. Create the code so that when the add button is clicked, the user is prompted for an item name, an item quantity, and an item price. Calculate the item total, and add it to the Subtotal field of the user control. Add the item name, the quantity, the price, and the item total to the list box. Continue this procedure each time the add button is clicked, and when all items are added, click the Calculate button of the user control to calculate sales tax and a grand total. Save all changes and exit Visual Basic.

PROGRAMMING AT WORK

In previous lessons of this workbook, you created a "card" class, representing a single playing card, and a "deck" class representing a deck of 52 playing cards. You use both of those classes in this project, in which you create a video game. In this phase of the card game project, you create the game board and implement the Concentration game. This game starts with a board where all 52 cards in the deck are displayed, facedown. The player overturns two cards. If both cards have the same value and same color suit, a match is made and the cards are removed from the board. If they do not match, the player turns the cards back over and tries another pair of cards. If the player is concentrating hard, he or she can remember where certain value cards are on the game board and can remove pairs quickly. The goal is to match all 26 pairs using as few comparisons as possible.

In this implementation of the game, the computer handles flipping the cards over. The backs of 52 cards are displayed, and the user clicks on two cards. When the first card is clicked, its face is displayed. When the second card is clicked, its face is displayed. When a Go! button is clicked, the comparison takes place. If a match is made, then these two cards vanish. Otherwise the backs of these two cards are displayed again. As the game proceeds, the total number of comparisons and matches are reported.

Begin by creating a folder named **CardGame3**. Open a new project, and name the form **frmConcentration**, and give it the caption **Concentration**. The form must be large enough to hold 52 small picture box controls, a menu, a couple of labels, and a command button. Set the Size property for the form to a value no smaller than **475, 650**. You can make it larger than that, but you need at least that much space to handle all of the controls without crowding them.

You need the two classes you created earlier, **clsCard**, and **clsDeck** for this project to work. Click the **Project** menu, select **Add Existing Item**, and then locate those two class files in the **CardGame2** folder from the workbook's Lesson 9 activities.

Create a menu named **Game** in frmConcentration. Add menu items **Play**, **Instructions**, and **Exit**. Each menu option should have an access key, and there is a separator before the Exit item. Add an ImageList control to the form. Select the **ImageList1** control, click the list arrow for the **Images** property, and find an image or icon that you want to use for the back of each playing card.

Add a PictureBox control to the form. You create a total of 52 picture boxes, so you need to choose a size that is large enough to see, yet small enough to fit all images into the form. Try a size around 30, 30 or 40, 40 to start with. Assign the image you selected for the ImageList control to the PictureBox control, and set the **SizeMode** property to **StretchImage**. Also, set the control's **BorderStyle** property to **FixedSingle**. You now need to make 51 copies of this picture box. Use Copy and Paste commands to create the copies, and then drag the copy to its proper location. Arrange the picture boxes as shown in Figure 11-1, in alternating rows of seven and six images. Once you get a row created, select, copy, and paste the entire row to speed up the process.

FIGURE 11-1
Arranging picture boxes
(*Note*: Figures 11-1 and 11-2 only show
the game area of the form. The title bar
is not shown in these figures.)

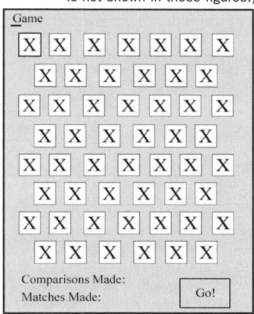

These picture boxes represent the backside of each of 52 playing cards. Once all the picture boxes have been created and placed, each of them has to be named. Starting at the top left of the form, name the leftmost picture box in row 1 **pic01**. The picture box to the right of it should be named **pic02**, and so on. Proceed left to right in each row. The lower–right picture box should end up as **pic52**. This naming convention is very important. The last two digits of these names are extracted and examined in the code to make the program work correctly.

Once the picture boxes are all created, placed, and named, you need to perform the same operation using Label controls. Add a Label control to the form. Clear the Text property if you want, but it is not essential, as the Text property is set in the code when the label is selected. Make the Label control the same size you specified for the PictureBox controls. Set its BorderStyle property to **FixedSingle**. Position the label over the top of the upper-left picture box so it hides the image used in the box. You now need to make 51 copies of this Label control, and position a copy on top of each of the remaining picture boxes, as shown in Figure 11-2. These Label controls are used to represent the face of each card and display the value and suit of each card when the card back is clicked.

FIGURE 11-2
Adding labels

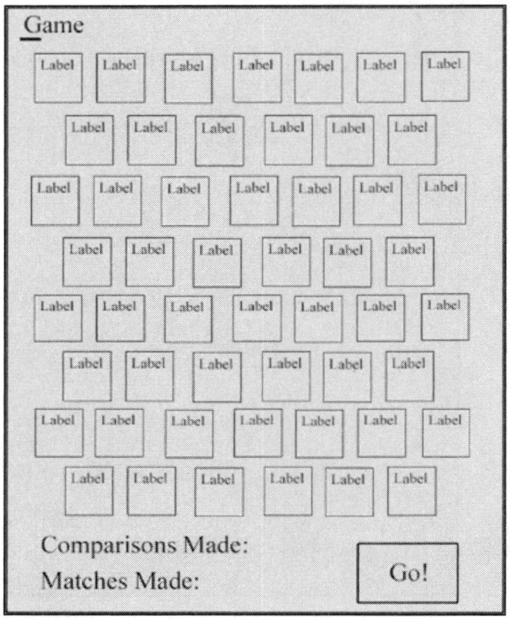

As with the picture boxes, once all the labels have been placed over top of the picture boxes, you need to name them using a similar naming scheme. The upper-left Label control should be named **lbl01**, the one to the right of it should be **lbl02**, and so on down to **lbl52**. An optional step is to physically place the labels behind the picture boxes, so when you view the form in Designer mode, you see the backs of the cards instead of the fronts. You can do this by clicking the upper-left label to select it, then press and hold down the **Shift** key, and click each of the remaining labels. When they have all been selected, click the **Format** menu, click **Order**, and then click **Send to Back**. The labels disappear and the picture boxes are visible.

At the bottom of the form, add two more labels, one named **lblComparisons** with a Text property of **Comparisons Made:**, and the other named **lblMatches** with a Text property of **Matches Made:**. Use a font and font size of your choice. Finally, add a command button named **btnGo** with the caption **Go!**

It is time to begin writing the code to implement the program! One important fact to keep in mind throughout the implementation is that the deck of cards is numbered from 1 to 52. The labels and the picture boxes are named from 1 to 52 as well. Therefore, you do not have to do any manipulation of index values when obtaining a card to display for a label.

Code the Exit menu option so that it terminates the program. Then declare five variables in the Declarations section of the code: **objDeck**, **intFirstCard**, **intSecondCard**, **intComparisons**, and **intMatches**.

Add code to the Play menu option that makes all the labels representing faces of cards invisible, and all the images representing backs of cards visible. You can do this with a For Each loop that loops through the form's Controls collection. If the type of object is a label, make it invisible and if the type of object is a picture box, make it visible. However, this also makes the two labels at the bottom of the form invisible as well. After the loop completes, reset **lblComparisons** and **lblMatches** to **Visible.** It is more efficient to let the loop make all labels invisible and then reset these two afterward. You could add logic to the For Each loop to look for those two labels and not make them invisible, but those comparisons would have to be done with each pass through the loop. So, overall, it is more efficient to just reset them when the loop ends.

The Play menu option event handler also must shuffle the deck, set **intComparisons** and **intMatches** to zero, and set **intFirstCard** and **intSecondCard** to -1. A value of -1 for these last two variables indicates that no selection has been made yet in the current selection of two cards. Also set the caption of lblMatches to **Matches Made: intMatches**, and similarly for lblComparisons. Add code to the Form_Load method to create the deck of cards and call its Initialize method, and then call the mnuGamePlay_Click event.

You now need to create a custom Click event handler to handle the clicking of the card backs. When the user clicks one of the PictureBox controls, you have to flip that card over to show the label side of the card.

But, you have 52 picture boxes. You do not want to create 52 Click event procedures, but a custom event handler can do what you need it to do. Create the event handler by coding the following statements:

```
Private Sub CardBack_Click(ByVal sender as System.Object, _
                          ByVal e as System.EventArgs) _
        Handles pic01.Click, pic02.Click, pic03.Click, pic04.Click,
pic05.Click, _
                pic06.Click, pic07.Click, pic08.Click, pic09.Click,
pic10.Click, _
                .
                .    'pic11 through pic50 statements coded in this
area
                .
                pic51.Click, pic52.Click
```

Now, when the user clicks one of the PictureBox controls, the name of that control is passed to the above event handler as the sender parameter. You need to define an Index variable and a Control variable that is used in a For Each loop in this event handler. When this event handler is called, it must first check to see if intFirstCard is equal to -1. If so, then this is the first card the user has selected. Use the Val and Mid functions to convert the last two digits of the sender.Name property to an integer value and store it in intFirstCard. Use this statement:

```
intFirstCard = Val(Mid(sender.Name, 4, 2))
```

If the control clicked was pic32, then intFirstCard ends up with a value of 32 after executing that statement. You must also assign the value of intFirstCard to the Index variable you created for this procedure as well. intFirstCard and intSecondCard must be retained until the cards are flipped back, or taken off the board in the event of a match. The Index variable is used in this event handler for the For Each loop, which is addressed momentarily.

If intFirstCard is not equal to -1, then the first card has already been processed. If intSecondCard is equal to -1, then this is the second card selected by the user. Perform the same processing for intSecondCard that you did for intFirstCard. If neither intFirstCard or intSecondCard is equal to -1, then the user has already selected two cards and is trying to select a third. Issue a message telling the user that they must click the Go button to proceed and process the two cards already selected.

Once the Index variable has been set to the value of either intFirstCard or intSecondCard, it is time to flip that card over. You use two For Each loops for this purpose. The first For Each loop searches the Controls collection looking for objects of type PictureBox only. When a PictureBox is found, use the following statements to compare the last two digits of its name to the Index value, substituting whatever names you declared for your local variables, and then making the control invisible and exiting the loop.

```
If  (Val(Mid(CtrlObj.Name, 4, 2))) = intIndex Then
   CtrlObj.Visible = False
   Exit For
```

Following that For Each loop, create another For Each loop to process the label controls and make the appropriate label visible. Use the same type of statement as shown above to convert the label name to an integer value for the comparison, and when the correct label is found, you must assign a card value to it, and make it visible, then exit the For Each loop. Use the following statement, or something similar, to assign the card value to the label:

```
CtrlObj.Text = objDeck.DisplayCard(intIndex)
```

You now need to create the Go_Click event handler code to process the cards that have been selected when the user clicks the Go button. Declare two String variables to hold the string representation of the two cards. Check that two cards have been selected (again use the fact that both intFirstCard and intSecondCard must not be equal to -1). If the user has not yet selected two cards, display a message and exit the subroutine. Otherwise, for the moment, flip the cards back over by making the images visible and the labels invisible. You flip the cards back over by making another For Each loop similar to the one used in the PictureBox control's Click event handler. Examine the control names and compare the last two digits of each picture box or label control to the values contained in intFirstCard and intSecondCard. You can create one loop to process both controls, or create two loops as done before. If you create one loop, be sure you process both the label and the picture box for the given Index value.

Finally, reset the variables intFirstCard and intSecondCard to -1 . Now you can test your program to make sure the things you have programmed so far are working correctly. Run the program. Click a card. The card should be displayed. Click another card. A second card should be displayed. Click on **Go!** The card backs should be displayed. Try clicking Go! with no cards flipped over. Select one card and then **Go!** Try selecting three cards before clicking Go! Try clicking on the same card twice. Since the label's Click method has no code, nothing should happen (which is what you want!). All of these situations should work correctly. If they do not, correct any problems you found before continuing with the implementation.

Add the comparison code into the Go! button Click event handler, following the code that checks if intFirstCard = -1 and intSecondCard = -1, and the error message if either one is equal to that value. Since the comparison is made between the values of the two cards and the suits of the two cards, these components must be extracted from the string representation of each card. Declare appropriate variables in the procedure. Use the string functions to extract the first *two* characters on the left of each card's string representation as the value of the card and the one rightmost character as the suit into the variables you just declared. The reason for extracting two characters from the left is that this allows the case of a value of 10 to be handled correctly without using a special case. All the other values are simply the value character and a blank space. Because you compare the two values for equality and have used the same extraction method for both cards, if the value is the same, the equality test returns True. The following is a sample of one method of obtaining the values in their proper format:

```
strFirstCard = objDeck.DisplayCard(intFirstCard)
strValueFirstCard = Trim$(Mid(strFirstCard, 1, 2))
strSuitFirstCard = Trim$(Mid(strFirstCard, 3))
```

Compare the values and suits of the two cards for a match. The suits match if one is hearts and the other diamonds, or if one is spades and the other clubs. The easiest way to do this is to create two Boolean variables to act as flags. Initialize both flags to False. If the values for card one and card two match, set the corresponding flag to True. If the suits match, set the corresponding flag to True. If both flags are True, there has been a match. In this case, increment the number of matches by one and modify the caption for lblMatches. Next, check if the player has won the game, i.e. made 26 matches. If so, display a congratulatory message. Finally, remove the cards by making the corresponding labels and images invisible. Do this using another For Each loop to check for controls of type PictureBox or Label, compare the last two digits of each control of those types to the intFirstCard and intSecondCard Index values, and make both the picture box and the label control invisible, which effectively removes them from the board.

If the cards do not match, flip the cards over. Because you have already written the code that flips them back over to test the program previously, simply cut and paste it into the correct position in the code. After the comparison of the cards has been made and handled, increment the comparison counter and update the lblComparisons' caption.

You should now have a functional game! As always, it is important that you test the program thoroughly. The easiest way to test this program is to comment out the line of code that shuffles the deck. Then the cards are laid out in the standard order on the display, so you know where the matching and non-matching cards are. Test matching cards and nonmatching cards. Cases you should be sure to test are cards that match where the first card has a suit of hearts and the second diamonds, and then where the first card has a suit of diamonds and the second hearts. Do a similar test for cards with spades and clubs. Also verify that cards with the same value but nonmatching suits do not get counted as a match. Be sure to also check that the cards with a value of 10 match correctly. If not, you may have to use a checkpoint and the debugger to examine the code that extracts the string value and suit from the card. Remove all the cards to verify that the winning message is displayed. Once you have removed them all, select **Play** from the **Game** menu and check that the cards are displayed again. After you have thoroughly tested your program in this way, remove the comment from the line that shuffles the deck, and see how many comparisons *you* take to win the game!

The final step in this project is to add a form containing the instructions that are displayed when the Instructions option is selected from the Game menu. Name the form **frmInstructions**, and give it the caption **Concentration Instructions**. Put a command button at the bottom with the caption **OK**, and unload the form when it is clicked. Put labels on the form containing the instructions. Run the program again and verify that this works.

UNIT 3 REVIEW

TRUE/FALSE

Circle T if the statement is true or F if the statement is false.

T   F   1. The StatusBar control can be divided into a number of panels that can be used to convey different information to the user.

T   F   2. A user control is easily identified because it does not contain any Toolbox components, such as buttons, labels, or text boxes.

T   F   3. A Windows Control Library project creates a DLL file, which stands for Dynamic Load Library.

T   F   4. The TreeView control is used by Windows Explorer to display a list of items in one of four different views.

T   F   5. Every time you create a new Windows Control Library project, Visual Basic automatically creates a default user control named UserControl1.vb.

T   F   6. The SmallChange property of the TrackBar control determines how far the thumb moves when the Page Up or Page Down keys are pressed.

T   F   7. A user control can be prepared for execution by building it from the Build menu or from the Debug menu.

T   F   8. The panels in a StatusBar control can be accessed using the PanelNum property of the Panels collection.

T   F   9. The ImageList control is one example of a control with no visible presence.

T   F 10. The pointer to the root node of a tree can be found in the TopNode property of the TreeView control.

MULTIPLE CHOICE

Select the best response for the following statements.

1. When viewed in the Object Browser, what icon appears next to the name of a variable that is not accessible to the application using the control?
   a. an X
   b. a circle with a slash through it
   c. a padlock
   d. an asterisk (*)
   e. a pound sign (#)

2. The use of what types of controls ensure that functions are used consistently among applications and also ensures they cannot be modified by the applications?
   a. inherited
   b. static
   c. user controls
   d. locked
   e. none of the above

3. Which TrackBar property determines the value of each tick mark on the trackbar's scale?
   a. MarkFrequency
   b. TickMarkFrequency
   c. ScaleFrequency
   d. ScaleRange
   e. TickFrequency

4. Any variables declared in the Declarations section of a user control are available to the application program as long as they are declared using
   a. the *Public* or *Dim* keywords.
   b. the *Public* keyword.
   c. the *Static* keyword.
   d. any variable declaration keyword except *Private*.
   e. the *Dim* keyword.

5. What word describes an item in the tree metaphor that is neither a root nor a leaf?
   a. parent
   b. sibling

    c. orphan

    d. branch

    e. none of the above

6. What keyword is used in an event procedure to cause the value of a variable defined with that keyword to retain its value beyond the end of the procedure?

    a. *Const*

    b. *Retain*

    c. *Static*

    d. *Global*

    e. *Permanent*

7. Which dialog box would you use to insert a user control created in a Windows Control Library project to a new or existing application project?

    a. Add New Item

    b. Add Existing Item

    c. Add DLL

    d. Add User Control

    e. Add Reference

8. The taskbar that is normally displayed at the bottom of the Windows desktop is an example of which of the following Visual Basic controls?

    a. StatusBar

    b. TaskBar

    c. TrackBar

    d. ProgressBar

    e. ProgramBar

9. Which of the following terms describes a process used in many companies where a programmer meets with other programmers to describe a new application and explain how the logic works?

    a. pass around

    b. flow meeting

    c. run by

    d. walk-through

    e. code session

10. The buttons Add Root and Add Child can be found in which of the following dialog boxes?

    a. TreeCollection Editor

    b. TreeNode Editor

    c. Node Editor

    d. Tree Editor

    e. NodeCollection Editor

FILL IN THE BLANK

Complete the following sentences by writing the correct word or words in the blanks provided.

1. In the _____ view of the ListView control, items are displayed with a small icon, the name of the associated item, and information about the size and the type of file or folder.

2. The original parts of a user control cannot be modified in a(n) _____ control.

3. The position of a StatusBar control on a form can be changed using its _____ property.

4. A DLL created by a project can be used in some other project by locating it in the _____ folder of the original project.

5. Visual Basic's System._____ class contains the tools and methods needed to create a user-drawn control.

6. Every node in a tree is a programmable structure that belongs to a(n) _____ collection.

7. When a new user control is added to a project, it always appears in its own _____.

8. When the _____ property of a PictureBox control is set to StretchImage, the image contained in the box expands or shrinks to fit the confines of the control.

9. To build a user control that can be used in other applications, you must first create a(n) _____ project.

10. When an item from a TreeView control is newly selected, a pointer to the node is passed as a parameter to the _____ event handler.

UNIT 4: ORGANIZING DATA, PROVIDING HELP, AND BUILDING APPLICATIONS FOR THE INTERNET

LESSON 12   **STACKS AND LISTS**

LESSON 13   **GRAPHICS, HELP, AND DEPLOYMENT**

LESSON 14   **CREATING WEB PROJECTS**

UNIT 4 REVIEW

LESSON 12   STACKS AND LISTS

TRUE/FALSE

Circle T if the statement is true or F if the statement is false.

T   F   1. A stack is a first-in, first-out method of organizing data in which items are added at one end and removed from the opposite end.

T   F   2. Many Stack classes have an operation called *peek*, which allows you to view the top element on the stack without removing it from the stack.

T   F   3. When a stack reaches its initial capacity, the most efficient method of increasing its capacity is to add one new element whenever it is required.

T   F   4. Many implementations of a Stack class also include some type of pointer to point to the top of the stack.

T   F   5. An attempt to pop an element from the top of an empty stack results in a run-time error.

T   F   6. When an expression is shown in infix notation, the operators are placed behind the operands to which they apply.

T   F   7. If a program processes the string expression 3 5 · 4 2 - +, the value on top of the stack when the expression has been processed is the value 17.

T   F   8. If you use the ReDim command to increase the size of an existing stack, the current entries in the stack are always saved and copied to the new and larger array.

T   F   9. The peek method reads the value on the top of the stack, and then decrements the top-of-stack pointer to point to the next element in the stack.

T   F   10. You can expose all of the elements of an array stack to a program by defining a public function in the Stack class that returns an array data type as its return value.

T   F   11. In the business world, most application programs are only used for a very short period of time so there is little need to add extensive documentation to a program.

T   F   12. The Contains() method of the Queue class is passed to an Object parameter, and returns the index of the entry within the queue if the object is currently contained in the queue.

T   F   13. The queue data structure is often used in simulation programs to simulate some event or situation.

T   F   14. A linked list structure requires one large contiguous block of memory to hold all items to be contained in the list.

T   F   15. Once memory is allocated for a linked list element, it is retained as long as the program is executing.

T   F   16. The operation used to remove an item from a stack is called a *pull*.

T   F   17. Postfix notation is also commonly called Reverse Polish Notation.

T   F   18. When parsing numbers from an input string, the space character is frequently used to indicate the end of an entry.

T   F   19. The first stacks were implemented in hardware and the stack was actually wired into the CPU.

T   F   20. The statement `Dim StackB As New Stack(StackA)` creates a a stack named StackB with the same capacity as StackA but does not copy the data elements from StackA to StackB.

MULTIPLE CHOICE

Select the best response for the following statements.

1. Which of the following is *not* an operation that is commonly used in stack processing?
   a. support for recursive functions
   b. passing parameters
   c. calling functions and procedures
   d. storing subsequent keystrokes while waiting to process previous characters
   e. interpreting expressions

2. Which term is used to describe a procedure or a method used to create a new instance of a class?
   a. instantiator
   b. originator
   c. constructor
   d. initiator
   e. none of the above

3. Which function can be used to resize a stack array when its maximum capacity has been reached and a new element needs to be added?
   a. ReSize
   b. ReBuild
   c. ReInit
   d. ReAlloc
   e. ReDim

4. The Stack class discussed in the text contained which of the following methods that can be called to clear all stack elements?
   a. Clear
   b. Purge
   c. Init
   d. Erase
   e. none of the above

5. Which of the following pointer types is pushed onto a stack when one method or procedure calls some other method or procedure?
   a. call protocol
   b. program flow
   c. return address
   d. flow routing
   e. send to

6. What term refers to the process of interpreting an input string into data and instructions?
   a. delimiting
   b. parsing
   c. deconstructing
   d. analyzing
   e. dissecting

7. Which method belongs to the String class and can be used when processing an expression to break the expression string into individual pieces?
   a. Break
   b. Split
   c. Divide
   d. Segment
   e. Dissect

8. When a Stack class uses a top-of-stack variable pointer, to what does the variable point?
   a. It always points at the beginning of the stack, for example, index location 0 in an array implementation.
   b. It points at the last entry that was added to the stack.
   c. It points to the last element available for storage. In an array implementation, it points to index $n - 1$ where n is the total number of elements in the array.
   d. It points to the next available location in the stack, for example, the first open element in an array version of a stack.
   e. none of the above

9. When defining a Stack class, or any class, you can create multiple methods with the same name by
   a. adding an underscore and a numeric suffix to each one, such as Build_1, Build_2, etc.
   b. altering the data type of the return variable for the method
   c. specifying different parameter types and numbers used as input to the method
   d. both b and c
   e. none of the above

10. Which of the following data types can be specified in a function declaration to return an array to the calling program?
    a. Object
    b. Array
    c. Structure
    d. Indeterminate
    e. General

11. A data structure that allows access to the structure from the front and from the back of the structure is a(n)
    a. stack.
    b. circular stack.
    c. snake.
    d. archive.
    e. queue.

12. Which operation of the Queue class is used to remove an item from the queue?
    a. Dequeue
    b. Unqueue
    c. Pop
    d. Remove
    e. Pull

13. Which of the following are required parameters for the CopyTo() operation of the queue structure?
    a. the location of an array into which to copy items
    b. the location of an array into which to copy items, and a starting index value
    c. the location of an array into which to copy items, a starting index value, and an ending index value
    d. the location of a queue into which to copy items
    e. the location of a queue into which to copy items, and the number of items to copy

14. Which item correctly indicates the minimum type of information that must exist for every element of a linked list?
    a. a data area
    b. a data area and a pointer to the previous element in the list
    c. a data area, a pointer to the next element in the list, and a pointer to the previous element in the list
    d. a data area and a pointer to the next element in the list
    e. none of the above

15. Which name is commonly used to refer to a variable that points to the first node in a linked list structure?
    a. top of list
    b. first node
    c. list head
    d. list start
    e. list begin

16. A linked list structure can be used to implement a(n) _____ if the nodes are always added to and removed from the front of the list.
    a. queue
    b. stack
    c. priority queue
    d. both a and c
    e. none of the above

17. What Visual Basic value can be used to initialize the pointer to the beginning of a linked list to indicate the list is currently empty?
   a. Nil
   b. Empty
   c. Zero
   d. Clear
   e. Nothing

18. Which of the following is a constructor type that creates a new instance of an object from an existing instance?
   a. copy
   b. duplicate
   c. replicate
   d. clone
   e. mirror

19. How many ways can the Visual Basic New constructor be used to create an instance of a stack?
   a. 1
   b. 2
   c. 3
   d. 4
   e. 5

20. Which keyword is used with the ReDim command when resizing a stack to ensure that the current stack entries are copied to the new stack?
   a. Retain
   b. Preserve
   c. Copy
   d. Keep
   e. none of the above

MATCHING

Write the letter of the description in the right column that defines the term in the left column.

_____ 1. postfix notation expression	a. Operation used to add an element to a queue
_____ 2. pop	b. Structure that uses a FIFO processing strategy
_____ 3. enqueue	c. Operation used to add an element to a stack
_____ 4. linked list	d. $a + b * c / d$
_____ 5. queue	e. Operation used to remove an element from a queue
_____ 6. infix notation expression	f. All of the elements of a stack
_____ 7. stack	g. A structure consisting of one or more nodes, each of which are allocated only when needed
_____ 8. dequeue	h. $6\ 2\ /\ 4\ 5\ 2 * + -$
_____ 9. body	i. A structure that uses a LIFO processing strategy
_____ 10. push	j. Operation used to remove an element from a stack

FILL IN THE BLANK

Complete the following sentences by writing the correct word or words in the blanks provided.

1. The operation to add an element to a stack is called a(n) _____.

2. The elements that make up a stack are sometimes referred to as the _____ of the stack.

3. The value returned from a stack pop operation is the object at the _____ of the stack.

4. The Stack class does not allow you to peek at the value at the top of the stack if the stack is _____.

5. A(n) _____ expression places the operators between the operands to which they apply, such as $a + b - c$.

6. A(n) _____ is often used as the character to denote the end of an input string when the string is being processed.

7. If an array to be used as a stack is declared as a(n) _____ variable in the class definition, it cannot be accessed directly from outside the class.

8. The space pointed to by the _____ pointer is always considered to be empty, whether it actually is or not.

9. Testing each new method or function of a program as it is created, and then moving on to the next portion of the program is called _____ programming.

10. When the name of a function is followed by empty parentheses, it indicates that the function does not receive any _____ when it is called.

11. A queue data structure is one example of a(n) _____-in, _____-out data structure.

12. The _____ operation is used to add a new item to a queue.

13. The queue structure operation that returns the value of the item at the front of the queue without removing the item from the queue is the _____ operation.

14. Every element in a linked list is referred to as a(n) _____.

15. The process of visiting every element in a linked list structure is referred to as a(n) _____.

16. In the implementation of the stack discussed in the text, the value returned from the _____ method is the value at the top of the stack.

17. An expression written in _____ notation has the arithmetic operators (+, * /, etc.) written behind the operands instead of between the operands.

18. A line of people at an airline counter waiting to be serviced is an example of a(n) _____.

19. The statement `Dim thisStack as New Stack()` creates a stack with a default capacity of _____ elements.

20. When creating a Stack class or a Queue class, it is possible to have multiple constructors with the same name as long as the _____ for each constructor are different.

WRITTEN QUESTIONS

Write a brief answer to the following questions.

1. How is the data in a stack organized? Describe the insertion and removal of data to and from a stack.

2. Describe the differences between an original stack, which was actually wired into the hardware, and a modern software implementation of a stack.

3. Visual Basic has a Stack collection that can be used in Visual Basic programs. Describe the three constructors available for the Stack collection and how each is used to create a stack, including any parameter input. Provide a code example of the declaration statement for each constructor.

4. What type of error occurs if a stack becomes full and a program tries to add another item, and how can this be fixed? What happens if a stack is empty and a program tries to remove an item, and how can this be fixed?

5. If a stack does become full during processing, does the program have to stop executing, or can the stack be enlarged? If so, how does the program do that? What happens to the existing elements?

6. What is the purpose of the peek operation of the Stack collection?

7. Describe how stacks are used to control program flow, such as when one method or procedure calls some other method or procedure.

8. Explain the difference between infix and postfix notation. Show an example of a simple expression in both formats.

9. Describe how a program uses the stack when parsing and processing the following expression 5 5 + 6 * 8 2 / -.

10. Describe the advantage(s) of using postfix expressions versus infix expressions.

11. The text for this lesson described the implementation of a Stack class. Describe in detail how the push, pop, and peek operations function for that class.

12. How does a queue structure differ from a stack structure?

13. Are items added to and removed from a queue using the same operations as a stack, namely push and pop? If no, what operations are used for the insertion and removal of items or elements to a queue?

14. Explain whether a stack or a queue would be best suited to handle the following two types of operations. Explain why in each case.

    a. inputting a series of numbers from the keyboard that are to be displayed in the same sequence they were entered after the last number has been entered

    b. inputting a series of numbers from the keyboard that are to be displayed in the reverse sequence they were entered after the last number has been entered

15. What is the purpose of the following Queue collection operations, and describe any parameters passed to or from each of the operations: Contains, CopyTo, and ToArray.

16. Give a brief description of a linked list and of what it is composed.

17. What are the possible advantages to using a linked list to implement a stack or a queue as opposed to an array?

18. How do you implement a stack using a linked list? Describe how nodes can be added to or removed from the stack.

19. Can a linked list be used to maintain an ordered list of items, that is, keep a list of items in numeric or alphabetic sequence? If so, how would you insert a new value into an existing list of values?

20. Regarding linked list processing and structures, what is a list head?

PROJECT 12-1

The text mentioned that a stack can be used to reverse the order of a string. One possible use for this process is to determine if an expression is a palindrome. A palindrome is an expression that reads the same backward as it does forward. It could be a single word, such as "otto," or the famous expression associated with Napoleon, "able was I ere I saw elba." In this project you create a program using the Stack class to test an expression entered by the user, then parse the expression, and then indicate to the user if it is or is not a palindrome.

Start a new Visual Basic project and name it **Palindrome** in a folder of the same name. Change the Text property of the form to **Test For Palindrome**. Add two labels to the top of the form and set the Text properties of the labels to **Enter an expression and click the Test button**, and **The program will determine if the expression is a palindrome or not.** Add a text box below the two labels, name it **txtInput**, and clear the Text property. Add three buttons below the text box, and name the buttons **btnTest**, **btnClear**, and **btnExit**. Change the Text properties of the buttons to **Test For Palindrome, Clear Input Box**, and **Exit**. Add one more label below the buttons, name it **lblResult**, and clear its Text property.

Enter code for the btnTest Click event to determine the length of the string entered by the user. Use string functions to extract each individual character from the input expression and push each character onto the stack as it is pulled from the string. After all characters have been pushed onto the stack, pop the top character and compare it to the first character in the original expression. If not equal, enter a message into the lblResult Text property indicating that the expression is not a palindrome, and exit the event procedure. If it is equal, pop the next character from the stack and compare it to the next character in the original expression. Continue the process until either a character from the stack does not match a character in the expression or the end of the stack entries are reached. If all characters match, enter a message into the lblResult Text property indicating the expression is a palindrome. Enter code for the btnClear Click event procedure to clear the text box and the lblResult Text properties. Enter code for the Exit button to end the application. Test the program with several expressions that are and are not palindromes.

(*Hint*: When extracting the characters from the expression to push onto the stack, use the Ucase function to convert the character to uppercase. When popping the characters from the stack to compare to the original expression, use the Ucase function again on the characters in the original expression to ensure they are in the same format as the saved characters. Remember, when comparing characters, an *a* is not the same as an *A*.)

PROGRAMMING AT WORK

In this project you create a project that uses a queue to store items for a To Do list. Create a new Visual Basic project and name it **ToDoList** in a folder of the same name. Change the Text property of the form to **To Do List**. Add three buttons and two labels to the form. Position the buttons one on top of the other near the center of the form. Position the two labels at the bottom of the form, one positioned below the last button, and the other label below the first label. Name the buttons **btnBuildList**, **btnGetTask**, and **btnExit**. Change their respective Text properties to **Build My To Do List**, **Get Next Task**, and **Exit**. Enter **Your Next To Do List Task Is:** as the Text property of the upper label. Name the lower label **lblTask** and clear its Text property.

Declare a queue capable of holding 10 items at the top of the program, using the Queue class. In the Click event procedure for the **btnBuildList** button, you prompt the user to enter a task to be performed, and ask them to assign a priority code to the task from 1 to 10. The lowest number (1) is the highest priority task to be performed, and the highest number (10) is the lowest priority task to be performed. Each priority code can only be assigned to one task and the program must check to be sure the user does not assign two different tasks the same priority code. If they do, they must reenter the code. The user can enter the task and associated priority code in any order. When the user is done entering data, you add the tasks to the queue in the proper order.

Declare an array of type String with 10 elements. Initialize each element to a null string value so you can detect a filled slot from an empty slot. Create a loop that prompts the user to enter a task and then assign an available priority code to it. Within the main loop, create an inner loop that builds a string variable indicating which priority codes are available. It loops through the array and if an array element is empty, the priority code for that slot would be the array index plus one. That value is then concatenated to the string variable, along with a space following the value, and then the loop examines the next slot in the array. When this loop completes, if the string variable is empty, then all the slots in the array are filled and the main loop must be stopped as no more entries can be added.

(*Note*: The first time the priority code list is shown, it says something like, *Choose a priority code from these choices: 1, 2, 3, 4, 5, 6, 7, 8, 9, 10*. If the user enters a task and then enters the priority code 4, the next time you build and display the priority code list it should say *Choose a priority code from these choices: 1, 2, 3, 5, 6, 7, 8, 9, 10*. Each time the user selects a priority code to associate with a task, that code is then removed from the list the next time it is displayed. The wording of the message is up to you. It does not have to be the exact text shown here.)

Otherwise, display a message asking the user to enter a task to be added to his or her To Do list. Give the user the option of entering a value to terminate the process, such as End, Quit, or Exit, or something similar. Continue to prompt the user for a task until some string is input or the loop termination value is entered. Once a string has been entered, and the loop is not being terminated, ask the user to choose a priority code from the list of available codes you built earlier. Make certain the value they enter is within the range of the array (1 to 10 in "relative to 1" terms), and is not a value that has already been entered for some other task. Display an appropriate error message if the user has entered some incorrect or duplicate value. When a valid task and priority code have been entered, store the task in the proper slot in the array (priority code value minus 1 is the correct array index), and return to the top of the loop to rebuild the list of still available priority codes.

When the main loop is terminated, either because the user entered the termination keyword or the array is full, enqueue each array item to the queue beginning with the index = 0 value. When the user clicks the Get Next Task button, dequeue the topmost item from the queue and display it in the lblTask Text property. Check to see if the queue contains any items before attempting the dequeue operation. When the queue is empty, place a message indicating that fact in the lblTask Text property field.

Save the program and test it thoroughly. Test with the maximum number of tasks (10), test it with only one entry, try to add duplicate priority codes, try to enter a null string as a task, a nonnumeric value as a priority code, a priority code out of the valid range, or any other condition you can imagine. When done testing, save any final changes you may make and exit Visual Basic.

LESSON 13   GRAPHICS, HELP, AND DEPLOYMENT

TRUE/FALSE

Circle T if the statement is true or F if the statement is false.

T   F   1. Most modern software is delivered with physical documentation manuals that are used extensively by the users of the software.

T   F   2. You can add a ToolTip control to a project by dragging the control from the Toolbox to the form.

T   F   3. When you dynamically define a ToolTip control using a code statement, the statement must be coded in the general declarations area.

T   F   4. You can change the ToolTip associated with a control anytime while the application is running.

T   F   5. The AutoPopDelay property of the ToolTip determines how long the pointer must remain in the ToolTip region before the ToolTip will display.

T   F   6. When using the pen component of the Graphics methods, you can only define one pen per application, but you can change its shape and color whenever needed.

T   F   7. The statement to change the pen color for a variable named penColor from its current color to the color black could be written: `penColor = New(Color.Black)`.

T   F   8. The smallest possible screen element that can be used to represent a colored dot is called a pixel.

T   F   9. The System.Drawing library contains a type named Point, and each point has an x and a y component that specify the x and y coordinates of a point.

T   F   10. In regards to graphing coordinates, the upper-left corner of a picture control is addressed as the 1st row and the 1st column.

T   F   11. One factor to consider when converting a standard graph x and y coordinates to pixel coordinates is the number of pixels per unit compared to the number of units represented in the graph.

T   F   12. When you add a Help button to a form, the user can click on a control and then click the Help button to get information about that control, if the Help information has been defined for that control.

T   F   13. When a Help button is added to a form, the button is visible in the upper-right corner of the form when the program is run.

T   F   14. To provide pop-up Help for a particular control on the form, you must enter a text string into the control's HelpText property that is displayed when the Help button is clicked, and when the control is clicked.

T   F   15. One advantage to storing Help information in Web pages on the Internet is that it makes it easy to provide up-to-the-minute information to all users of the program without having to send them new Help files.

T   F   16. If an online Help file is defined when the Help system is activated, the default Web browser is started and the Help page is displayed.

T   F   **17.** Once the Help system for a form has been properly set up and the properties of the HelpProvider control have been correctly set, you can activate the Help system when one of the form's controls has the focus, and the F8 key is pressed.

T   F   **18.** The tags used to create HTML code are case sensitive and mixing the case for a starting and ending tag can cause major problems when the page is viewed.

T   F   **19.** When viewing a Web page in your browser, you can see the actual HTML tags that make up the page by selecting an option from the View menu that lets you view the HTML source code.

T   F   **20.** When trying to deploy a Visual Basic .NET application to another computer, the Packaging and Deployment Wizard guides you through the steps involved.

T   F   **21.** A .NET application can be deployed to another computer that supports the .NET architecture simply by copying the program's .exe file to the new computer.

MULTIPLE CHOICE

Select the best response for the following statements.

1. Which of the following terms refers to the process of moving an application program from one machine to another?
   a. cloning
   b. replication
   c. deployment
   d. propagation
   e. extraction

2. After adding a ToolTip control to an application, you use its _____ method to associate a particular control with a string of text that becomes its ToolTip.
   a. AddToolTip
   b. SetToolTip
   c. NewToolTip
   d. DefineToolTip
   e. CreateToolTip

3. Which of the following ToolTip properties determines if the ToolTip is or is not displayed when the mouse pointer hovers over its associated control?
   a. Visible
   b. Show
   c. Hide
   d. Active
   e. Enabled

4. Which of the following ToolTip properties determines the amount of time a ToolTip remains visible while the pointer remains in the ToolTip region?
   a. AutoPopDelay
   b. InitialDelay
   c. ReshowDelay
   d. VisibleDelay
   e. EnabledDelay

5. Which component of the graphing methods determines the color and thickness of lines and shapes drawn by the Graphics methods?
   a. Stroke
   b. Fill
   c. Pencil
   d. Pen
   e. none of the above

6. Which of the following methods is used to invoke the Graphics methods that are used to draw shapes and text objects?
   a. Paint
   b. Draw
   c. Write
   d. Pen
   e. Display

7. Which of the following methods is used to force a picture box control to redraw itself?
   a. Paint
   b. Draw
   c. Refresh
   d. Repaint
   e. Display

8. Which Graphics method is used to draw a single straight line from a beginning point to an ending point?
   a. PaintLine
   b. DrawLine
   c. ShowLine
   d. Line
   e. CreateLine

9. Which Graphics method is used to draw a shape, such as a parabola, by drawing lines from point to point?
   a. PaintLines
   b. DrawLine
   c. ConnectLines
   d. Lines
   e. DrawLines

10. Which corner of a picture box control is considered the "origin" of the picture box as far as the Graphics methods are concerned?
    a. upper-left
    b. lower-left
    c. exact center
    d. upper-right
    e. lower-right

11. If a math graph spans 15 units along the *x* coordinate, how do you determine how many pixels are contained in a picture box for each math graph unit?
    a. multiply the width of the picture box by 15
    b. multiply the width of the picture box by 15 and add a value of 1 to the total
    c. the math units and the pixel units are the same in all cases, 15
    d. divide the width of the picture box by 15
    e. divide the width of the picture box by 15 and subtract 1 from the total

12. Which of the following buttons is replaced when a Help button is added to a Visual Basic form?
    a. Close button
    b. Minimize button
    c. Maximize button
    d. Options a, b, and c
    e. Options b and c

13. Which of the following controls can be added to your form when you want to incorporate a Help button in the application?
    a. HelpTip
    b. HelpButton
    c. HelpProvider
    d. HelpDialog
    e. HelpBox

14. What icon or character typically appears on a Help button to help a user identify it as a Help button?
    a. a capital "H"
    b. a lowercase "h"
    c. an exclamation point (!)
    d. a question mark (?)
    e. the word *Help*

15. Which term refers to a type of dialog box that cannot be closed until the user clicks one of its buttons?
    a. persistent
    b. modal
    c. direct-response
    d. response-required
    e. none of the above

16. Which property of the HelpProvider control must be set to a Web address or the path to a resident HTML file to link an application to an external help file?
    a. HelpNamespace
    b. HelpFile
    c. HelpURL
    d. HelpLocation
    e. HelpPath

17. Topic and Index are two possible settings for which property of the HelpProvider control?
    a. HelpKeyword
    b. HelpMethod
    c. HelpType
    d. HelpLocation
    e. HelpNavigator

18. Which of the following tag pairs are used to mark the beginning and the end of an HTML page?
    a. <body></body>
    b. <start></end>
    c. <html></html>
    d.
    e. <head></head>

19. In which Visual Basic directory should you store your application-resident Help files to ensure that the program can find them without difficulty?
    a. the folder where the source for the form and code are stored
    b. the Bin directory where the executable file is stored
    c. the Help folder
    d. the HTML folder
    e. the Debug folder

20. Visual Basic program source code is turned into which of the following intermediate languages before it can be executed?
    a. P-code
    b. byte-code
    c. pseudo-code
    d. MVBL
    e. MSIL

21. Which of the following files are required to be on any computer attempting to run a Visual Basic .NET application program?
    a. network.dll
    b. mscorlib.dll
    c. csc.exe
    d. all of the above
    e. options b and c only

22. Which section of an HTML page contains information about the page, including the title?
    a. <head>
    b. <body>
    c. <meta>
    d. <prefix>
    e. none of the above

MATCHING

Write the letter of the description in the right column that defines the term in the left column.

_____ 1. Refresh

_____ 2. DrawLine

_____ 3. AutoPopDelay

_____ 4. HelpProvider

_____ 5. HelpNavigator

_____ 6. Paint

_____ 7. Point

_____ 8. DrawLines

_____ 9. HelpNamespace

_____ 10. InitialDelay

a. Special data type of the System.Drawing library

b. Method used to draw parabolas generated by quadratic equations

c. Determines the amount of time the pointer must hover over a control before a ToolTip appears

d. Method used to force a picture box to repaint itself

e. Property used to link an application to an external Help file

f. Property that determines how the HelpKeyword is used

g. Method used to draw a line from endpoint to endpoint

h. Control that is used to connect a Help file to an application

i. Method used to invoke the Graphics methods to draw shapes and text

j. Determines how long a ToolTip remains visible when the pointer is in the ToolTip area

FILL IN THE BLANK

Complete the following sentences by writing the correct word or words in the blanks provided.

1. The yellow box that pops up when you hover the mouse pointer over a control, or a toolbar button, is called a(n) _____.

2. You can dynamically create a ToolTip control using the statement, `Dim MyToolTip as New` _____().

3. If you define a ToolTip control in a form's constructor, it must be placed under the Initialize _____() statement.

4. The _____ method, used to assign a ToolTip to a control, requires the name of the control and a text string as its input parameters.

5. The _____ property of the ToolTip control determines the amount of time before another ToolTip appears when the pointer is moved from one ToolTip region into a different ToolTip region.

6. The paint method has a special parameter (e of type _____), through which it is able to invoke the Graphics methods.

7. The term _____ is short for picture element.

8. The version of the DrawLine method used in the text requires four _____ data type parameters.

9. For each ordered pair of parameters sent to the DrawLine method, the *x* parameter represents the _____ value of the point, and the *y* represents the _____ value of the point.

10. In addition to the pen, the other parameter sent to the DrawLines method is an array of the _____ data type.

11. The row pixel coordinate in a picture box control gets larger proceeding from _____ to _____.

12. When you define a Help button for a form, you must set the MinimizeBox and the MaximizeBox properties of the form to _____.

13. When a Help button control has been added to a form, you must change the _____ property of the control from its default value of False to a value of True.

14. While pop-up Help allows you to provide limited help information, you can supply much more information using _____ Help which usually consists of Web pages, either on the Internet or resident in the application.

15. When Help is provided in the form of Web pages, each page can contain _____, which the user can click to go to a page with even more information on specific topics.

16. The HelpProvider control uses the control's _____ to locate a particular topic in a well-constructed Help file.

17. The KeywordIndex setting for the _____ property of the HelpProvider control specifies a keyword to search for and the action to take in the specified URL.

18. You can insert horizontal lines in a Web page to break the page into easily identifiable sections using the HTML <_____> tag.

19. You define a hyperlink to a Web page (or internal HTML page) by specifying the URL or the path name in the tag <a _____ = "page address">.

20. In order for a Visual Basic .NET program to be able to run on another computer, that computer must support the .NET _____.

21. Visual Basic .NET is considered a(n) _____-level programming language because it is easily understood by programmers.

WRITTEN QUESTIONS

Write a brief answer to the following questions.

1. What is the purpose of a ToolTip, and how does a user activate a ToolTip?

2. What does a ToolTip look like when it appears on the screen, and how does the user get rid of them once they appear?

3. What does the SetToolTip method do? What parameters are passed to this method, if any? Is there anything else required to use this method?

4. Describe the two ways that a ToolTip control can be added to a Visual Basic .NET project.

5. Describe the purpose of the following ToolTip control properties: Active, AutoPopDelay, InitialDelay, and ReshowDelay.

6. Describe the purpose of the Pen tool, and any parameters that are required to create it. Provide sample code statements for defining a pen and an associated color.

7. Can you declare more than one pen in any given application program? Explain.

8. What is the purpose of the Paint method?

9. What is a pixel and what is it used for?

10. Describe the DrawLine method and any parameters required to use this method. (*Note*: There are many variations of this method in various platforms. Describe the parameters required for the version of the method discussed in the text for Lesson 13.)

11. How does the DrawLines method differ from the DrawLine method? Are its parameters, as discussed in the text, different than the DrawLine method?

12. Explain the *x* and *y* coordinate system used to draw a graph in a picture box control as opposed to the *x* and *y* coordinate system used to draw a math graph.

13. What is the difference between online Help for a program and pop-up Help?

14. Does the addition of a Help button to a form have any affect on other form controls?

15. What do you have to do to add pop-up Help for a control on a form? How does the user activate the pop-up Help information?

16. Is there any advantage to using online Help versus pop-up Help?

17. If you want to use online Help in your application, how do you tell Visual Basic where the Help file is located?

18. What happens when an application is created using online Help and the user asks for help for a particular control?

19. What are the HelpProvider's HelpKeyword and HelpNavigator properties used for?

20. Explain the purpose of the following HTML tags: <html></html>, <head></head>, and <body></body>.

21. What is MSIL?

PROJECT 13-1

Copy the contents of the folder named **EnterOrder** that you created in Project 11-2 to a new folder named **EnterOrder2**. In this project you are going to create ToolTips for the controls on the form for this application. Start Visual Basic and open the **EnterOrder** project from the **EnterOrder2** folder you just created. Add a code statement to the general declarations area declaring a ToolTip control named **OrderTips**. Add the following statements to the form's Load event procedure to define ToolTips for the controls on the form:

```
OrderTips.SetToolTip(lstOrderItems, "Items you enter will display here.")
OrderTips.SetToolTip(btnAddItem, "Click this button to enter an item.")
OrderTips.SetToolTip(btnExit, "Click this button to exit the program.")
```

Build the program and run it. Move the pointer over each of the above controls to display your ToolTip. If a ToolTip is not displayed, check your code for errors and try again. When these ToolTips are working correctly, add ToolTips for the controls in the Sales Tax user control. You need to open that control in its Code window, and declare a new ToolTip named **TaxTips**. Then enter code statements in the Load event procedure for the control to provide ToolTips for the **lblSubTotal**, **lblTax**, **lblGrandTotal**, and **btnCalculate** controls. Use the text shown below for those controls. You then need to rebuild the Sales Tax control and rebuild the overall project. Run the program and make sure all of your ToolTips are displayed properly. Save all changes and exit Visual Basic.

Text to enter for Sales Tax controls ToolTips:

lblSubTotal - *The order subtotal will display here as items are entered.*

lblTax - *The sales tax will display here when the total is calculated.*

lblGrandTotal - *The final total will display here when the Calculate button is clicked.*

btnCalculate - *Click here to finalize your order.*

PROJECT 13-2

In this project you modify an existing application to use pop-up Help instead of using ToolTips. Copy the contents of the **EnterOrder2** folder you created in Project 13-1 to a new folder named **EnterOrder3**. Open the project and delete all of the ToolTip code from the Sales Tax user control and from the main form. Add a **HelpProvider** control to the main form. Click the form to select it, and set the HelpButton property to **True**. Set the MinimizeBox and MaximizeBox properties to **False**. Click on each of the controls on the form and enter a text string into the HelpString property for each control. Open the Code window for the Sales Tax user control and add descriptive text for each of the output labels and the Calculate button. Rebuild the control and the entire project and run it. Click the **Help** button and click on one of the controls to see the help string associated with that control. Click away from the control, click the **Help** button again, and click on another control. Continue this process until you have seen the help string displayed for each control on the form (other than the text labels, although you can add Help for them to if so desired). Save all changes and exit Visual Basic.

PROJECT 13-3

In this project you use the DrawRectangle Graphics method to draw a sequence of squares of decreasing size. The DrawRectangle method requires five parameters: a pen, a starting *x* coordinate, a starting *y* coordinate, the width of the rectangle, and the height of the rectangle. Start a new Visual Basic project and save it with the name **DrawSquares**. Change the Size property of the form to **320, 340**. The default form is 300 by 300, but that entire area is not really accessible. The title bar takes up some of the vertical space, and you cannot quite use all of the horizontal space, either. Create a Click event handler for the form by entering the following code:

```
Private Sub Form1_Click(ByVal sender As Object, ByVal e As System.EventArgs)
                    Handles MyBase.Click
    Form1.ActiveForm.Refresh()
End Sub
```

Now, create a Paint event procedure by entering the code shown below. This block of code defines a pen with a color of red and a line thickness of 2. There are four Integer data types defined for the starting coordinates and the width and height coordinates. A while loop then calls the DrawRectangle method repeatedly to draw squares of ever decreasing size until the width variable reaches a value of 10.

```
Private Sub Form1_Paint(ByVal sender As System.Object, _
        ByVal e As System.Windows.Forms.PaintEventArgs) Handles MyBase.Paint
        Dim drawColor As Color = Color.Red()
        Dim drawPen As New System.Drawing.Pen(drawColor, 2)
        Dim x As Integer = 5
        Dim y As Integer = 5
        Dim xWidth As Integer = Form1.ActiveForm.Size.Width - 20
        Dim yHeight As Integer = Form1.ActiveForm.Size.Height - 40

        While xWidth > 10
            e.Graphics.DrawRectangle(drawPen, x, y, xWidth, yHeight)
            x += 10
            y += 10
            xWidth -= 20
            yHeight -= 20
        End While
    End Sub
```

Run the program and see the squares get smaller and smaller, giving an illusion of depth to the form. Now, modify the program so it rotates different colors for each drawing cycle. You can do this any way you choose. You could set up an array of colors and loop through the array selecting a different color each time, or you could add a loop counter to the while loop and set up a case statement that determines a color based on the value of the while loop, or even use a random number generator to set a color. Don't forget to change the pen to the new color before making the drawing. When your changes are in, run the program and examine your results.

PROGRAMMING AT WORK

In the final project for this lesson you convert an application from pop-up Help to online Help. Copy the contents of the **EnterOrder3** folder to a new folder named **EnterOrder4**. Before opening the Visual Basic project, you need to create an HTML Help file. Open a text editor program and enter the statements shown below to get the HTML file started. This set of statements starts the HTML file and creates a small heading section that contains only the title that appears in the browser's title bar. The body section uses the H1 header format (the largest HTML heading) to show the same title in the body of the page. The <hr> tag is used to draw a horizontal rule, or line, across the page. The size=10 attribute sets the thickness of the line. The noshade attribute specifies that the line is a solid black line. The remainder of the HTML statements are inserted after the <hr> tag and before the </body> tag that ends the main body of the page.

```
<html>
<head>
<title>Order Entry Help Page</title>
</head>
<body>
<h1>Order Entry Help Page</h1>
<hr size=10 noshade>

</body>
</html>
```

Next, you set up a series of hyperlinks to the topics that are contained in this HTML file. Enter the following set of statements following the <hr size=10 noshade> statement:

```
<h2>Click one of the hyperlinks below to view text concerning that
control.<h2></a>
<hr size = 3>
<a href=#itemlist>Order Items List Box</a><br>
<a href=#additem>Add Item Button</a><br>
<br>
<hr size=10 noshade>
```

If you examine the <a href= statements you see that they look different from the hyperlink statements shown in the main text. The pound sign (#) following the href= attribute indicates to the Web browser that the target of this link resides in this file. The pound sign indicates a named location within this file to which the browser jumps when a user clicks the link. Unlike the Help file you created in the Step-by-Step exercise, this Help file contains all of the Help information in one file, but you create a link from the top of the page to each individual topic. The above block of code shows links to only two of the topics you need. Create additional hyperlink statements using the following location names and hyperlink text. Insert the additional hyperlinks following the <a href= statement for the additem location. Model the new statements after the two shown above. The <br> after each link forces the following link to the next line in the Web page. The <hr> at the end draws another horizontal line to act as a separator between the links and the topics to follow.

```
#exit - Exit Button
#subtotal - Subtotal Field
#salestax - Sales Tax Field
#grandtotal - Grand Total Field
#calculate - Calculate Button
```

Now, you are ready to define the Help topics themselves. One advantage to online Help is that you can provide a lot more detailed information than you would normally want to provide in a ToolTip or a pop-up Help string. Enter the code shown below to define the Help topic for the order item list box. Note the first line is another anchor tag (<a>), but this tag uses the name= attribute instead of the href= attribute. This tag is assigning a name to this location in the file, and this tag name matches the name in the first href= statement you entered earlier. The name in the href= statement was preceded by the pound sign (#), while the name= tag encloses the name in double quotation marks. This is how the browser finds the location denoted by the href hyperlink tag. The first statement also sets the text to the H1 format to make it stand out, and with one additional twist it also uses the <font> tag to change the heading text to a blue color. A line break follows the header (note that the font and the h1 closing tags follow the text itself) and then the descriptive text for the item list box is provided. A paragraph break <p> follows the last line of text. The last tag in this set is to draw another horizontal line, but this time with a thickness of 5 instead of 10.

```
<a name="itemlist"><h1><font color=blue>Order Items List Box</font></h1></a>
<br>
The Order Items List Box is used to show you the items you have ordered. Each
time you add an item to your order it creates a new row in the Order Items
List Box containing the name of the item, the quantity you ordered, the unit
price for the item, and the total price for the quantity you ordered.
<p>
<hr size=5 noshade>
```

Using the above code block as a guide, create the Help topic sections for the remaining items. Be sure that the name= text matches the href= text in the original hyperlink statement, or the browser cannot find the link target. Provide any information for each of the remaining controls that you think is relevant and can help a user when they have a problem or question about the control.

Save the HTML file as **OrderHelp.htm** in the Bin folder of the **EnterOrder4** project folder. Before attempting to incorporate this file with the Visual Basic project, open your Web browser and load this page. Click the **File** menu, then select the **Open** or **Open Page** (options vary depending on the browser being used), locate the Bin folder for this project, and select the **OrderHelp.htm** file to be opened. If you see any problems, correct them in the text editor, save the file, and click the **Reload** or **Refresh** button on your browser to load the updated page. When the page appears correct to you, close the browser and open the Visual Basic project.

Click the **HelpProvider** control, and then select the **HelpNamespace** property. Enter **OrderHelp.htm** in the Namespace field. Select each of the controls on the main form, and delete the HelpString property text strings. Change the HelpKeyword values to match the topic headings used above. For example, the Help-Keyword value for the Add Item button would be **Add Item Button**, as shown in the beginning set of code for this project. Change the HelpNavigator property to **AssociateIndex** if it is not already set to that. Access the form for the Sales Tax user control, and add the **OrderHelp.htm** filename to the **HelpNamespace** property for that HelpProvider control. Again, select each of the controls that has a HelpString defined and delete the string. Set the HelpKeyword properties for the controls and the HelpNavigator property if necessary. Rebuild the user control and the project, and then run the project. Click the **Help** button, and click on one of the controls. Your Web browser should start and display the OrderHelp.htm page you just created. Click the hyperlinks for your Help topics and you should jump to that section of the page.

Users may want to browse multiple Help topics when they get to this page. It would make the page easier to use if they could return to the hyperlink list at the top of the page after reading each individual topic. Open the **OrderHelp.htm** page in a text editor and add the following statement at the top of the page, immediately following the first <hr size=10> tag following the <h1> heading line:

```
<a name="top">
```

That tag assigns a name to the top of the page that can be referenced after each topic. Now, add the lines below after the <p> paragraph tag following each Help topic. The first line references the top tag you just entered, and the text (in red) tells the user they can return to the top of the page by clicking the hyperlink.

```
<a href=#top><font color=red>Go to top of page</font></a>
<br>
```

Save your changes, test them in a browser, and then rerun the Visual Basic project. Test your top of page links to be sure they function correctly, and that the other hyperlinks still work as well. When satisfied that all is right, close the project and exit Visual Basic.

LESSON 14   CREATING WEB PROJECTS

TRUE/FALSE

Circle T if the statement is true or F if the statement is false.

T   F   1. Creating Web pages using HTML requires the use of special HTML editing software.

T   F   2. You can add interactivity and functionality to a Web page by using a scripting language in conjunction with HTML statements.

T   F   3. CGI is a scripting language that runs on the client computer.

T   F   4. ASP .NET is a platform from which Web application programs are run.

T   F   5. ASP .NET requires the use of Visual Basic or some other Visual Studio component.

T   F   6. Aside from using a different template to create the project, there is no difference between an ASP .NET application and a standard Visual Basic Windows application.

T   F   7. The type of client computer and the operating system settings on that computer can affect the visual appearance of a Web page.

T   F   8. If you make a change in one view of the Web form designer, such as Grid layout view, the changes are not visible in the other view until you rebuild the project.

T   F   9. In grid layout mode for a Web form, you can type text directly into the designer window and the text is displayed in the same location when the page is opened in a Web browser.

T   F   10. The files for an ASP .NET Web application must reside on the server, and cannot be saved in any folder of your choice.

T   F   11. You can view your page as it would appear in a browser at any time by clicking the Browse button at the top of the Designer, but it does not show your latest changes unless you rebuild the project first.

T   F   12. You can change the width of the border around an HTML table with the cellBorder= attribute.

T   F   13. The HTML controls added to a Web page in grid layout mode have added functionality for use in ASP applications.

T   F   14. You can add a table to a Web form page in grid layout mode and then switch to flow layout mode to modify the table.

T   F   15. You can convert an HTML control to a server control with the statement, type="server".

T   F   16. Web application server pages are all stored in the wwwroot directory.

MULTIPLE CHOICE

Select the best response for the following statements.

1. HTML is an acronym for
   a. Hyperlink Manager Language.
   b. Hypertext Modeling Language.
   c. Hypertext Markup Language.
   d. Homepage Making Language.
   e. none of the above.

2. The computer used to process Web page requests is called a
   a. Web client.
   b. Web spinner.
   c. Web reader.
   d. Web server.
   e. Web router.

3. Which of the following scripting languages run on the client computer?
   a. CGI
   b. Perl
   c. BasicScript
   d. Java
   e. JavaScript

4. What does the acronym ASP stand for?
   a. Active System Processor
   b. Active Server Pages
   c. Active Script Processing
   d. Active System Programming
   e. Active Script Pages

5. In order to run ASP .NET applications, you must have access to a Web server configured with which of the following server software components?
   a. MIS
   b. ADO
   c. IIS
   d. ISW
   e. SIS

6. Objects created from the ASP .NET _____ class are containers for controls and for HTML code.
   a. Page
   b. Object
   c. Component
   d. System
   e. Framework

7. The controls and graphic elements for a Web form are saved in a file with which of the following extensions?
   a. .vb
   b. .wfp
   c. .wp
   d. .aspx
   e. .aspf

8. The Web application Designer view that allows you to see the HTML code is called _____ layout mode.
   a. grid
   b. code
   c. tag
   d. HTML
   e. flow

9. The controls that are added to a Web form are called _____ controls.
   a. Web
   b. active
   c. passive
   d. server
   e. dynamic

10. In grid layout mode, what do you have to do to position text where you want it to appear when the page is displayed in a browser?
    a. Select the Text tool and type the text where you want it to be.
    b. Position a Text control on the page and enter the text.
    c. Position a standard Windows application Label control on the page and then enter the text.
    d. Switch to flow layout mode, enter the text, switch back to grid layout mode, and drag the text to the desired position.
    e. Position an HTML label control on the page and enter the text.

11. Which section of the Toolbox contains the Horizontal Rule control?
    a. Web Forms
    b. HTML
    c. General
    d. Web Page
    e. Other Controls

12. What file extension does the code-behind file have?
  a. .aspx
  b. .cbf
  c. .vb
  d. .cod
  e. .cb

13. Which attribute of the HTML <table> tag determines the amount of space between the table cells?
  a. cellSpacing
  b. cellPadding
  c. cellGap
  d. cellBorder
  e. cellSeparation

14. When a control is added to a Web page in grid control mode, part of the style value determines the exact position of the control, which is known as _____ positioning.
  a. relative
  b. exact
  c. grid
  d. absolute
  e. precision

15. To be able to change a control in response to some user event, you must be able to identify the control in program code, which you can do by assigning an identification attribute to the control using the _____ tag.
  a. name=
  b. id=
  c. tag=
  d. idtag=
  e. codename=

16. Which of the following statements could you code to declare a new table row object to an HTML table?
  a. dim newRow as New HTMLRow()
  b. dim newRow as New Row()
  c. dim newRow as New HTMLTableRow()
  d. dim newRow as New HTMLTable.Row()
  e. dim newRow as New TableRow()

17. Which of the following items are part of an ASP .NET application?
  a. controls used to build Web pages
  b. objects used to build Web pages
  c. a run-time system that executes pages on a Web server
  d. both a and b
  e. a, b, and c

18. While the controls and graphic elements of a Web form are contained in one file, the code that is executed for the form is contained in a separate class file with which of the following file extensions?
  a. .aspx
  b. .cls
  c. .asp
  d. .vb
  e. none of the above

MATCHING

Write the letter of the description in the right column that defines the term in the left column.

_____ 1. Web server

_____ 2. Web forms

_____ 3. HTML

_____ 4. grid layout

_____ 5. HTML controls

_____ 6. platform

_____ 7. server controls

_____ 8. IIS

_____ 9. flow layout

_____ 10. ASP .NET

a. Platform from which Web applications are run

b. The combination of hardware and software on which an application program runs

c. Controls run on an Internet server after the page has been posted to the client computer.

d. A server software package that is required to run ASP .NET application programs

e. A Web application Designer view that shows the HTML statements for the page

f. Objects created from the ASP .NET Page class.

g. Language used to build Web pages

h. Controls on a Web page that are not actively managed by an Internet server

i. The place where a Web page is built before it is sent to a Web browser that requested the page

j. Web application Designer view that shows the page as it appears when displayed in a browser

FILL IN THE BLANK

Complete the following sentences by writing the correct word or words in the blanks provided.

1. You can see the source tags used to build a Web page by clicking the Source or Page Source (depending on the browser) option from the browser's _____ menu.

2. Most Web pages created with standard HTML tags are _____, meaning they do not move or change dynamically.

3. Even though the Web browser used to view a Web page runs on the client computer, any changes to the appearance of the Web page must be processed on the _____ server.

4. The combination of hardware and software on which application programs are run is called a(n) _____.

5. ASP .NET uses _____ .NET for database access.

6. The Visual Basic _____ that opens for a Web application looks different than the one that opens for a Windows application.

7. When a user requests a Web forms page from a Web server, the page is run through the ASP .NET _____ to build the page before it is sent to the user.

8. The Web application Designer _____ layout mode is also referred to as the "what you see is what you get" mode.

9. _____ controls differ from those added to a Windows form because they are run on the Web server after the Web page has been posted to the client computer.

10. To see how your Web form appears in a browser, you can right-click the .aspx file in the Solution Explorer, and then click the _____ option to compile the page and display it as it appears in a browser.

11. When creating a Web application, the code that is shown in the _____ window is the code that is executed on the server when the Web page responds to some user action or event.

12. In the Designer, you can switch to flow layout mode from grid layout mode at any time by clicking the _____ button at the bottom of the window.

13. The _____ attribute of the HTML <table> tag determines the amount of space between the cell's content and the cell border.

14. You can turn an HTML control into a server control by setting the control's _____ attribute.

15. You can set a Date control to the current date with the statement `Dim thisDate As Date =` _____ .

16. You can display a date with the month spelled out by using the _____ date parameter of the Format function.

WRITTEN QUESTIONS

Write a brief answer to the following questions.

1. Where are Web pages on the Internet stored, and what happens when you request one through your Web browser?

2. What is a scripting language and for what is it used? Identify at least two scripting languages.

3. What is ASP and how do those pages differ from a standard HTML page?

4. Can anyone create ASP .NET applications or are there special requirements to create these types of pages?

5. Is there any difference in creating a Visual Basic Windows application project versus creating a Web application project?

6. Describe the two views available in the Web application Designer.

7. What is the difference between a server control and a standard Toolbox control added to a Windows application?

8. How can you add text to a Web application in grid layout mode and have the text appear in the same position when the page is viewed in a browser?

9. You have opened a Web application project and added several controls to the form. You click the Browse tab at the top of the Designer window to see how your form looks in a Web browser, but none of the controls you have added are visible. Why?

10. Is there any way to convert an HTML control into a server control? If so, how?

11. Write the HTML tag required to begin a table for a Web form. Set the amount of space between the cells to four pixels, and the amount of space between the cell border and the cell content to five pixels. Define a border for the table that is eight pixels wide, and make each column of the table 100 pixels wide. Include the code required to convert the table to a server control with an id of tblDemo.

12. How would you create a new project but include a Web page that exists in another project in the new project?

PROJECT 14-1

While Active Server Pages are an integral part of developing a Web application using VB .NET software, ASP applications existed prior to the new release of Visual Studio. Using the Internet, or a library, do some research on ASP. When was it first introduced as a viable concept? For what types of applications is it used? What does the future hold regarding ASP? Search for information on these questions, and any others you may think of that you think may provide useful information on the topic to yourself or your classmates. Write a short report describing the results of your research. Be prepared to report your findings to your classmates.

UNIT 4 REVIEW

TRUE/FALSE

Circle T if the statement is true or F if the statement is false.

T   F   1. The term pixel is short for picture element, and it represents the smallest screen element that can represent a colored dot.

T   F   2. A platform is defined as the hardware that makes up a specific computer.

T   F   3. In programs that parse input strings, a period is often used as the string terminator character.

T   F   4. There are three types of controls that can be added to a Web form: server controls, Action controls, and HTML controls.

T   F   5. The AddToolTip method is used to associate a control with a string of text about the control.

T   F   6. A queue structure is a last-in, first-out type of structure.

T   F   7. To create a new Web application project, click the File menu, then Project, and then select the ASP .NET Web application icon in the Templates pane of the New Project Window.

T   F   8. You can call the Redraw method of a picture box control to force the control to redraw itself.

T   F   9. The flow layout mode of the Web application designer is also referred to as "what you see is what you get" mode because it shows how the page looks when viewed on the Web.

T   F   10. In order for users to use an application with online Help, they must first start their Web browsers before starting the application program.

T   F   11. The procedure or method used to create a new instance of a class is called a constructor.

T   F   12. The memory required for a linked list structure must be allocated when the program begins execution.

MULTIPLE CHOICE

Select the best response for the following statements.

1. What is the small yellow box called that appears when you hover the mouse over a control or a menu button?
   a. StickyNote
   b. HelpHint
   c. ToolTip
   d. ToolCue
   e. HelpCue

2. Which of the following scripting languages normally runs on the Web server where the Web pages being processed are stored?
   a. CIG
   b. CGI
   c. JavaScript
   d. VBScript
   e. Java

3. Which function is used to insert an item into a queue?

   a. push

   b. pull

   c. enqueue

   d. dequque

   e. insert

4. Which term refers to the process of removing an item from a stack?

   a. pull

   b. peek

   c. push

   d. pry

   e. pop

5. When creating a new Web application project, which of the following names is the default name for the IIS server?

   a. webserver

   b. localhost

   c. wwwroot

   d. webroot

   e. webhost

6. Which ToolTip property determines the amount of time a pointer must hover in the ToolTip region before the ToolTip becomes visible?

   a. AutoMaticDelay

   b. AutoPopDelay

   c. ReshowDelay

   d. InitialDelay

   e. StartDelay

7. When you are in flow layout mode of the Web application designer, how could you switch back to grid layout mode?

   a. Click the Design button at the bottom of the Designer window.

   b. Click the Grid View button at the bottom of the window.

   c. Click the View menu, and then click the Grid Layout option

   d. Double-click in the flow layout window to toggle back to grid view.

   e. Right-click the flow layout window and then select the Grid Layout option from the pop-up menu.

8. When adding pop-up Help to a control, which property of the control is used to contain the string of text to be displayed?

   a. HelpText

   b. HelpArea

   c. HelpString

   d. ControlHelp

   e. PopupHelp

9. Which expression format describes the expression A + B * C / D?
   a. postfix
   b. infix
   c. simple math
   d. prefix
   e. simplistic

10. Every element in a linked list is referred to as a(n)
    a. node.
    b. member.
    c. link.
    d. unit.
    e. entry.

11. When any user requests a Web forms page from the Web server, the Web server runs the page through the ASP .NET
    a. Decoder.
    b. Compiler.
    c. Framework.
    d. Parser.
    e. Server.

12. In addition to the pen, what other parameter(s) is sent to the DrawLines method?
    a. an array of the point data type
    b. the starting and ending x and y coordinates for the line
    c. the starting and ending x and y coordinates and the color of the line
    d. the color of the line
    e. the starting coordinates of the line, and the length and width of the line

FILL IN THE BLANK

Complete the following sentences by writing the correct word or words in the blanks provided.

1. To create an ASP .NET Web application program, you must have access to a Web server configured with Microsoft Internet _____ Services server software.

2. A(n) _____ operation is used to read the top element off a stack without removing it from the stack.

3. Setting the _____ property of a ToolTip to False means the ToolTip is not displayed when the pointer hovers in the ToolTip region.

4. Web forms are built from the ASP .NET _____ class.

5. A data structure that can be accessed from the front and the back of the structure, but items can only be removed from the front, is called a(n) _____.

6. The _____ method is used to draw a series of lines from point to point, such as a parabola or an arched line.

7. Every element in a(n) _____ data structure contains a data area and a pointer to the next element in the structure.

8. A stack can be dynamically resized using the _____ statement.

9. The controls and other graphic elements of a Web form are all stored in a file with a file extension of _____.

10. The process of moving an application program from one computer to another is called _____.

11. Interpreting a string entered by a user into data and instructions is called _____ the string.

12. To add pop-up Help to a Visual Basic program, you must first add a(n) _____ control to the form's component tray.